SECRETS OF THE NLP MASTERS

50 Techniques To Be Exceptional

Judy Bartkowiak

SECRETS OF
THE NLP MASTERS

50 Techniques To Be Exceptional

Judy Bartkowiak

First published in Great Britain in 2014 by Hodder & Stoughton. An Hachette UK company.

First published in US in 2014 by The McGraw-Hill Companies, Inc.

This edition published 2014

British Library Cataloguing in Publication Data: a catalogue record for this title is available from the British Library.

Library of Congress Catalog Card Number: on file.

Paperback ISBN 978 1 473 60012 6

eBook ISBN 978 1 473 60013 3

10 9 8 7 6 5 4 3 2 1

The publisher has used its best endeavours to ensure that any website addresses referred to in this book are correct and active at the time of going to press. However, the publisher and the author have no responsibility for the websites and can make no guarantee that a site will remain live or that the content will remain relevant, decent or appropriate.

The publisher has made every effort to mark as such all words which it believes to be trademarks. The publisher should also like to make it clear that the presence of a word in the book, whether marked or unmarked, in no way affects its legal status as a trademark.

Every reasonable effort has been made by the publisher to trace the copyright holders of material in this book. Any errors or omissions should be notified in writing to the publisher, who will endeavour to rectify the situation for any reprints and future editions.

Typeset by Cenveo® Publisher Services.

Printed and bound in Great Britain by CPI Group (UK) Ltd., Croydon, CR0 4YY.

John Murray Learning policy is to use papers that are natural, renewable and recyclable products and made from wood grown in sustainable forests. The logging and manufacturing processes are expected to conform to the environmental regulations of the country of origin.

John Murray Learning
338 Euston Road
London NW1 3BH

www.hodder.co.uk

CONTENTS

INTRODUCTION

NLP, or neuro-linguistic programming, has been defined and described as many different things, from a manual for the mind to a toolbox of techniques. Its positive focus and practical applications for all aspects of one's life have attracted interest from a wide age group. NLP is practised in front of huge audiences on stage and in schoolrooms, clinics and company boardrooms. Surely, this thing that provokes such an intense response needs further investigation. Where better to focus, then, than on the proponents of NLP, the NLP Masters. Who are they and what do they say?

This book is a collection of insights drawn from NLP writers, trainers, therapists, coaches and those they inspired, who either came from other disciplines or moved into them afterwards, and so drills into a rich reservoir of knowledge and experience.

Neuro-linguistic programming was developed by Richard Bandler and John Grinder in the early 1970s at the University of California in the United States. Maths student Bandler was transcribing some seminar sessions delivered by Fritz Perls (Gestalt Therapy founder) and Virginia Satir (Family Therapy founder) at the behest of Dr Robert S. Spitzer. He must have found them inspiring because he started copying what they taught and found he got the same results as they did. Spitzer even said, 'Richard spent several months transcribing the audio tapes and after a while developed many of Virginia's voice patterns and mannerisms.' Of Bandler's work with Perls he said, 'He came out of it talking and acting like Fritz Perls. I found myself accidentally calling him Fritz on several occasions.' What Bandler had done using his mathematical brain was to break down the structure and code of what they did so that he could reproduce it. This they called 'modelling', and this is essentially what lies at the core of NLP and is what makes it unique as a therapy.

The fact that this led to Bandler running therapy groups on the campus based on Satir's and Perl's work shows how absolutely he had modelled them. His activity attracted the attention of Grinder, a linguistics student, and he, too, started to get involved and bring to the table his expertise with words. By copying what Bandler said and did, he got the same results and together they published their first NLP book in 1975, *The Structure of Magic*. In the book they introduced their first NLP model, the Meta Model, which was based on the language patterns of Perls and Satir. It identifies 12 ways of challenging the deletions (vague speaking), distortions (mind-reading) and generalizations that can interfere with our ability to develop ourselves into the great people we want to be. You will become familiar with these interventions throughout this book.

Virginia Satir has been enormously influential in the world of NLP and specifically contributed the much-vaunted anchoring techniques, which you will get the chance to practise in many different contexts. She also introduced Bandler and Grinder to the representational systems – visual, auditory and kinaesthetic – that enable us to understand the different ways people make sense of their world and choose to communicate it to others. By matching them, we can gain understanding of and rapport with others.

Grinder and Bandler also modelled the work of Milton Erickson, from which they developed the Milton Model. This took the deletions, distortions and generalizations of the Meta Model into hypnotic forms and metaphors, enabling us to gain greater understanding of how we perceive our world so that we can make changes to improve it. Milton shows us how the very vagueness that can interfere with clear and resourceful communication when used in a hypnotic form can encourage people to find the gaps in the content from their subconscious, where the deeper content lies.

What Grinder and Bandler wanted to do was model the excellence of these therapists so that it could be reproduced by anyone who used this code. In effect, they wanted to create a user manual for the mind. The benefit would be that by understanding how our thinking affects our language and actions to get a result, we would be able to change that result by changing the underlying thinking.

Thus, NLP is often seen as a collection of methods and models that we can use to understand our thought processes and behaviour and, by understanding them, change them (should we want to) to get the result we want. We call this the desired or compelling outcome. The chapter headings have been devised to represent and focus on possible desired outcomes that you might have, so find the ones that most resonate with you.

Here is how Bandler and Grinder describe NLP – note their emphasis on curiosity and exploration (key drivers in NLP), and on the desire to understand the other person's map of the world (how they make sense uniquely of events and experiences, feelings and communication).

> **'NLP is an attitude which is an insatiable curiosity about human beings with a methodology that leaves behind it a trail of techniques.'** Richard Bandler

> **'The strategies, tools and techniques of NLP represent an opportunity unlike any other for the exploration of human functioning, or more precisely, that rare and valuable subset of human functioning known as genius.'** John Grinder

Others who were influential in the early days of NLP were Judith DeLozier and Robert Dilts. We will be using Dilt's Neurological Levels of Change model several times in this book, as well as DeLozier's work on reframing. Both of these enable us to make significant changes in our life while remaining true to our values and identity. Working with John Grinder, they developed New Code NLP in the 1980s, which focused on the relationship between conscious and unconscious processes. It works more with engaging the unconscious mind through using metaphors (where one thing represents another), patterns, time frames, logical levels and perceptual positioning, all of which are described and used several times through this book.

Since then, many NLP Masters have added to this, with further work on metaphors and 'clean language' by David Grove and by those who modelled his original work – Penny Tompkins and James Lawley. NLP has been applied to every area of life and has spread all over the world.

Fundamental to NLP is the idea of modelling excellence: the idea that, if someone else can do a thing, then by coding it, being curious about the structure of this thing and taking on the underlying belief, then we too can do that thing. I would encourage you to embrace a state of curiosity as you read this book. What could you learn? What could you add to your skill set?

There are 50 chapters, many on a similar theme, so you can pick and choose those that best relate to your desirable outcome. Each one offers different examples of how to apply techniques and some will be more relevant than others. Examples span areas such as health, weight loss, business, parenting, sport and relationships. Some of these will be more relevant than others but the themes can be applied in other contexts. For example, you may not want to lose weight but you might want to reduce your drinking or smoking, so the chapter will still be relevant. You may not be in a relationship at the moment but you will still have relationships you value with friends or colleagues, siblings and parents.

You will find some repetition of techniques, albeit using different contexts, and this is deliberate. This means that, if you've selected specific chapters, you will not have to flick back through the book to find where a technique is explained.

In each chapter there are quotes from NLP Masters, some of whom are well known, others less well known. They are chosen more because they seem to make a good point well rather than because they are necessarily considered to be an NLP Master, although most of them are. Many are from Sue Knight who trained me and whom I consider to be a model of excellence as an NLP writer. Many of the NLP Masters wrote books based on therapy, some of which are almost verbatim reports on therapy sessions, which, while they make fascinating reading, don't necessarily provide pithy quotes. Therefore the absence of quotes from certain NLP masters whose work you may admire is not because I do not rate their work but rather because I could not find suitable quotes that were short or expressive enough to include. Quotes were chosen carefully to give you cause for reflection. Many do not even come from the world of NLP but nevertheless express a view that I consider pertinent to the chapter.

There are a number of presuppositions or beliefs about life that Bandler and Grinder found were inherent in their models of excellence in those early days, and even more than a quarter of a century after their initial work they strike a chord with us to the extent that, when we take on these presuppositions, things change for the better, we feel empowered and resourced. A list of these, then, is my gift to you at the start of this book. Read the book believing the following presuppositions to be true and suspend your scepticism and those limiting beliefs that usually prevent you from achieving what you want:

- Everyone makes the best choice available to them – accept, understand and forgive.
- There is no failure, only feedback – accept mistakes as a learning opportunity.
- Behind every behaviour is a positive intention – be curious, find it and learn from it.
- The map is not the territory – what you feel is only one way of looking at things; there are other ways that might prove more useful.
- The meaning of the communication is its effect – take responsibility for what and how you communicate.
- We already have all the resources we need – tap into all your resources and divert them to where they are needed.
- The person with the most flexibility has the most influence – the more choices of how to respond we have, the better.
- Mind and body are one – what affects one affects the other.
- If one person can do a thing, anyone can – this is what modelling is for.
- There is a solution to every problem – be curious to find it.
- What is true of someone else is true for us, too – what we notice in others we have too; that's how we recognize it.
- If you always do what you've always done, you will always get what you've always got – it's you who have to change if you want a different result.

Which of these is the one that will make the difference for you? When we set about modelling the excellence of others, whether they be someone who has managed to overcome serious difficulties in their life, achieved great sports prowess or acting skill or is a great inspirational teacher, we can look at these presuppositions and consider which of them might have been true for that person.

It isn't just other people's excellence we can examine and copy but also our own. We all do things with excellence. However you may feel about certain aspects of your life, there will be parts of it where you think you have expertise and skills. When you focus on that skill, what belief do you hold? Which of those presuppositions is true for you as you use that skill? Which presupposition has to be in place for it to be possible to do that skill? Now, if you accept that you have that belief, you can start to be curious about where else that belief and that skill could be useful and be applied to great effect.

You see: you do have all the resources you need and this book is another resource for you to add to them.

This SECRETS book contains a number of special textual features, which have been developed to help you navigate the chapters quickly and easily. Throughout the book, you will find these indicated by the following icons.

 Each chapter contains **quotes** from inspiring figures. These will be useful for helping you understand different viewpoints and why each secret is useful in a practical context.

 Also included in each chapter are three **strategies** that outline the ways you can put this secret into practice.

 The **putting it all together** box at the end of each chapter provides a summary of each chapter, and a quick way into the core concepts of each secret.

 You'll also see a **chapter ribbon** down the right-hand side of each right-hand page, to help you mark your progress through the book and to make it easy to refer back to a particular chapter you found useful or inspiring.

12
13
14
15

1 Set a realistic goal

 'The greatest personal limitation is to be found not in the things you want to do and can't, but in the things you've never considered doing.' Richard Bandler

'If you think you can do a thing or think you can't do a thing, you're right.' Henry Ford

'A goal without a date is just a dream.' Milton Erickson

'You have to set goals that are almost out of reach. If you set a goal that is attainable without much work or thought, you are stuck with something below your true talent and potential.' Steve Garvey

 'All our dreams can become true if we have the courage to pursue them.' Walt Disney

The difference between a goal and a dream is reality. You can dream about becoming a bestselling writer, the CEO of your company, a famous actor, top athlete or getting to the top of your profession but, unless it becomes your goal, it will remain a dream.

Most people are probably familiar with SMART goals – goals that are specific, measurable, achievable, realistic and timed. We know that we need to be specific about what we want, and be able to measure it so we know when we have succeeded. It should be possible for us to achieve it ourselves or for us to learn how to do so from someone else, by modeling them. We should also name a date by which it will be complete, otherwise the goal becomes just a dream because there's no end to it.

So knowing this, why don't we then achieve our goals when we apply these simple rules? In this chapter we will look at one element – being 'realistic'. Firstly, what does this mean? One person's 'realistic' is not the same as another's. This is based on self-belief, the desire to achieve the goal, one's physical and mental abilities, and funds available. These things are generally set in the present. However, your goal will be achieved in the future, so you have the power to change all these factors such that it will be realistic. The secret of setting realistic goals is to be willing to suspend belief.

How helpful is it really that the goal should be realistic anyway? After all, if some of the famous explorers and adventurers had set only realistic goals, they would never have done the things for which they are now famous. After all, it was widely believed that the world was flat and that, if one were to sail to the edge, the ship would fall off the edge into, well, no one knew what, so it wasn't a realistic goal to aim to sail around the world. Yet, it was done. Until scientists find the cure for a disease, it is often believed to be incurable, so therefore off-limits as a realistic goal. Indeed, people have been cured by faith healers and indeed many other seemingly unrealistic methods. Magicians appear to do things that aren't realistic, and we are spellbound as we watch escapologists find a way out of seemingly impossible cages underwater or even walk on water.

So who is to say what is realistic? How important is it and does being realistic actually restrict us? Or does the fact that it restricts us enable us to achieve our goal? Maybe it depends how important it is to you, how much you want it and what you are prepared to do to achieve it.

The NLP Masters recommend that the goal needs to be possible or realistic in the sense that you can control the outcome. For example, explorers, scientists and entrepreneurs who have achieved impressive and groundbreaking objectives have been able to do so because they did not rely on other people and could control their outcome to some extent. Obviously, some factors are out of our control such as the weather, so in a sense no one has 100-per-cent control. We cannot control the feelings and behaviour of other people who could prevent us achieving our goal.

WHO'S DONE IT?

When you are testing your goal for being realistic, ask yourself who you know who has done this thing already, or something similar.

Read books and articles about people who have succeeded in doing something along the same lines as you're planning. Watch TV footage or YouTube videos and study how they do this: listen to what they say, paying particular attention to the difference that makes the difference for them. Maybe this might also be true for you?

Those people who have done what you want to do are your models, so break down what you learn to get the structure of their excellence so that you can copy it and have a go yourself.

When you are **modelling** people who have succeeded in achieving the goal similar to yours, pay particular attention to their belief. You will need to copy what they say and do and how they look when they're doing this thing, but their success will fundamentally come down to their belief about doing it.

It's quite difficult to guess someone's belief and, if you ask them, they don't always know or can't put their finger on quite what the belief is that makes the difference between success and failure for them. It might therefore be a matter of **TOTE – Test Operate Test Exit.** Try on one of their apparent beliefs for size. Say to yourself: 'When I believe XXXXX, what difference does it make?' You're acting as if this belief makes the difference. It may, it may not. In which case, you test again using another belief, until you get the desired result. The desired result may not be the goal in its entirety but may be an element of it or a skill you need to achieve it.

Reading people's autobiographies is usually a good way to get under their skin and discover their beliefs, so take the opportunity to read whatever they've written about themselves. Follow them on Twitter and 'like' their Facebook page to get further insight into how they think and to learn how you can incorporate their model to achieve your goal.

ASSESS YOUR SKILLS

What skills do you need to make your goal realistic? We can often get bogged down in detail. When we think of our goal, we might list all the things we need – money, skills, contacts, experience in this thing, and so on. We list the individual skills as detailed and specific, possibly too specific. Instead of being specific, ask yourself these questions.

1. What skills do you have currently? Make a list.
2. What are you good at? Make another list.
3. What do other people say you are good at? Another list.
4. What do you notice other people being good at? The fact that you notice these skills in other people indicates that you too have these skills. We say in NLP: 'If you spot it, you've got it.' So make a list of these skills, too.
5. What did you use to be good at? Another list.

Look at these lists and find the **patterns**. What sort of things do you seem to be good at? Put them into the following categories: Physical, Mental, Creative, Social.

Now we're going to **chunk up**. This means taking those things you are good at and asking you to take them up a level. So if you're good at these things, what does it mean you are? Can you think of a few words to sum up your strengths? Write them down.

Having chunked up, we're now going to **chunk back down** but with your goal in mind now. Thinking about these strengths and your goal, how easy will it be to achieve it? How can you apply each of these strengths to particular aspects of your goal? How will strength X help you? Which parts of achieving your goal will be assisted by this strength? Then move on to the next one until you've carefully plotted how each of these strengths will serve you in achieving your goal. How realistic does it now seem to you?

In the previous strategy we learned how we can use modelling to make our goal realistic by finding people who have the skills we will need. In this section we have learned how to take our existing skills and, by chunking up and down, discover how they can be applied to our goal in order to make our goal realistic.

RESEARCH + FEEDBACK

Sometimes goals need further **research** in order to find out what might be available to help you achieve them. Perhaps you will need specific equipment, clothing, training facilities, information and so on. You can't expect to achieve your goal without doing thorough research. Talk to people who have done this thing already and model them, using the modelling strategy outlined above. In addition, check out what could be happening in the field you are interested in so that you can take advantage of other people's work and build on it with their association and contacts.

Research the Internet for ideas. You may need technology to make your goal realistic and there is constant development in the area of technology all over the world. Maybe someone right now is working on something that would enable you to achieve your goal.

Question received wisdom – maybe your information is out of date. Remember, people once thought the world was flat and that you would fall off the edge if you sailed towards the horizon!

Feedback is very important in order to fine-tune your goal so that it is realistic. As you make headway towards your goal, notice the results you get and be curious. You won't be successful immediately, otherwise this isn't really a goal. It will take many attempts and some changes in approach based on feedback. Feedback is a learning opportunity. When things go wrong, what is this telling you? Each supposed 'failure' is giving you information on how to improve.

Putting it together

Be tenacious and take these learnings so that your goal becomes realistic. If you know that someone else has achieved a particular goal, it means that this goal is realistic and that you can achieve it too. What you have to do is model those who have achieved it, recognize and access your own skills and strengths, and use feedback in a positive way, questioning and researching information you can use to help you achieve your goal. Many people give up on their goal, saying 'It just can't be done' or 'it's not possible for me to do it'. Others, by putting no end date on it, keep it as their dream, never to become a reality.

2　Set a compelling goal

66 *'The difference between those who succeed and those whose goals last as long as a house built on sand lies in their willingness to pay the price. For example, are you willing to let go of everything you think you hold dear to achieve what you really want?'* Sue Knight

66 *'The future is a good place to get interested in because you're going to be spending the rest of your life there.'* Paul McKenna

66 *'Imagination rules the world.'* Benjamin Disraeli

66 *'Whenever you want to achieve something, keep your eyes open, concentrate and make sure you know exactly what it is you want. No one can hit their target with their eyes closed.'* Paulo Coelho

66 *'Change is the only constant in life. Are you going to choose the direction life will take and the kind of person you will become or will you just sit back and wait for life to happen to you?'* Richard Bandler

How important is it for you to achieve your goal? How much do you want it? A compelling goal is one that you will move heaven and earth to bring about. It's a goal that you will take risks to succeed at and make sacrifices for. 'Compelling' means that you are drawn towards it like a magnet, unable to resist its pull and the force of its attraction.

Goals can become burdens we carry around with us. They become part of our personality, our packaging, how people know us — for example, 'She's always on a diet', or 'He's trying to set up his own business', 'They're trying for a baby.' You are so much more than your goal, but so long as it's not actually happening you develop a sense of it being part of your identity. It affects everything you do and everything you are, how you relate to other people and how they relate to you. Because of this, sometimes there can even be a sense of loss or grief when you have achieved your goal because you wonder what comes next. It is so much a part of you that you start to question 'Who am I when I don't have this goal?' And, indeed, who are you? For example, when you are your goal weight, what next? Your identity was as a dieter and perhaps you associated with other dieters through a group. Will you still be a part of this group when you have achieved your goal? Perhaps you're trying to give up smoking. What will you do when your friends all go outside for a smoke? Will you miss this ritual? It is important that you set a goal that is compelling and which you want, despite the fact that you will be a different person when you've achieved it. Can you cope with this and the loss of the goal as an appendage?

ASSESSMENT: DO YOU HAVE A COMPELLING GOAL?

Test whether your goal is compelling by asking yourself these questions:

1. What do you really want? Choose something that really excites you.
2. What would you do if the world was going to end in a week? This puts you in touch with what's really important to you.
3. What would you do if you knew you couldn't fail?
4. Who wants this goal? Is it really 100 per cent your goal or is it something someone else thinks you should/must/ought to do?
5. What will having this goal give you? What values does it underpin for you? Values let you know what's important to you.

6. On a scale of 1–10, how important is this to you?
7. Who will you be when you have achieved this goal?
8. What will you no longer be able to do, once you have achieved this goal? Will that be a problem for you, or for other people you care about? How will you manage this?
9. When you imagine yourself achieving this goal, what do you see, hear and feel and what are you doing?
10. Go through this list again until you have **three** goals. Then prioritize which one to go for.

What counts as compelling, like beauty, is in the eye of the beholder. It is not your remit to fashion a goal that is compelling for others, for your family, your loved one, your boss or your department. The only way to create a compelling goal is to ask yourself how much you want it for yourself.

Truly compelling goals, goals that really resonate with who you are, are goals that are congruent with your values in life. Some of your values will have been inherited from your parents and others will have evolved from your subsequent life experiences. If you're not sure what your values are, then ask yourself: 'If the world was going to end in a week, what would I do?' This question tends to disclose our priorities in life – what has to be true for everything else to work. Another way of finding your values is to ask yourself: 'What makes me really mad and angry?' Think back to the last time you got very cross – what was it about? Focus on the underlying value that was not adhered to rather than the content of the story.

Our values make us who we are. By going for a goal that is truly in line with our core values, we become more of who we are. We consolidate our identity. Think about your identity and who you'll be when you meet your compelling outcome.

There are downsides to achieving your goal. Other people know and love us for who we are: the someone who is aiming for this goal. Will they feel the same when we have achieved it? Maybe they're going for the same goal and will be less successful in achieving it – how will that alter the dynamics of your relationship?

LOGICAL LEVELS OF CHANGE

We can use the Logical Levels of Change to explore how to make our goal compelling. Look at the Logical Levels diagram in the Appendix and think about your goal at the top of the triangle. Ask yourself the following questions:

1. Move down a level and ask yourself who that means you are. What is your identity as you reach for that goal, what does it need to be to attain it?
2. What values and beliefs will serve to underpin and drive you towards that goal?
3. What skills do you need to apply to achieve it?
4. What actions will you take?
5. How can you adapt your current modus operandi to accommodate your goal?

If you find at any level that there is some incongruence or misalignment, return to the previous level and repeat it. If necessary, you may need to go back to your goal and rephrase it to make it more compelling or even change it completely.

Only when you can move fluidly through the levels from top to bottom and back up again, with each level fully aligned, will you know that your goal is really compelling.

ANCHORING

A great thing to do when you have a fully aligned compelling goal is to anchor a visualization of you having achieved it. The reason we want to do that is to be able to keep on track when the going gets tough, which it will if our goal is really something worth going for.

So, close your eyes and think about you achieving your goal. Make it present by imagining that right now you have achieved it, that you are that person:

- What can you see? Picture it in glorious Technicolor.
- What can you hear? Pump up the volume.
- What is happening? Make this an action movie.
- How are you feeling? Be aware of your whole body.

When all your senses are alive with the thrill of the experience of you having achieved your goal, squeeze your earlobe and hold it there while you enjoy the sensation. As the senses diminish a bit, release your ear and 'break state'. That means we just give ourselves a shake and move about a bit to ease the tension.

To get the association between the sensation and the action of squeezing your earlobe, you need to do it a few times. You can alter the images and sounds to experience different aspects of achieving your goal but make sure you maximize each sense.

Once the sensation and action are fully associated, you will be able to repeat the action of squeezing your earlobe anywhere and at any time to remind yourself of what it feels like to have achieved this compelling goal.

Putting it all together

It is easy to get caught up in media hype and pressure from friends and family as well as from your work environment and social network, and to form goals that fit with other people's needs and expectations of you. These are not compelling goals. They are not goals that will work. You may achieve them but they fall short of what you are capable of. Instead, use the strategies above to form compelling goals – goals that you feel proud to be associated with, goals that inspire you and drive you towards them because they put a fire into your breast as you think about how you will feel when you have achieved them.

When your goal is compelling, you will be motivated and focused even when people try to distract you from it. You will know that this goal fits with your values and beliefs and will confirm your identity and purpose.

3 Reframe the goal

> 'Reframing enables you to put a new or different frame around an image or experience. What seems to be an extremely challenging situation in the present can be reframed to have less impact when considered as part of your whole life experience.' Mo Shapiro

> 'We have the mental tools and skills to get rid of the crap we don't want and replace it with what we do want. You can be whoever you choose to be.' Richard Bandler

> 'A signal has meaning only in the frame or context in which we perceive it.' Tony Robbins

> 'Many fables and fairy stories include behaviours that change their meaning when the frame changes. The different-looking chick seems to be an ugly duckling. He has been comparing himself to all the other ducks and now he is a beautiful swan.' Dr Lisa Christiansen.

> 'Take that which you no longer need, bless it for what it has done for you, and then set it free.' Virginia Satir

The meaning of an event depends on how we frame it. When we change the frame, we change the meaning. For example, the event of slipping on a banana skin is very different depending on whether you are the observer or the victim.

A QUESTION OF PERSPECTIVE

Imagine you are in an art gallery and looking at a painting. You can look at it from many vantage points and each will give you a slightly different perspective. Right up close and you won't see a thing (and the alarm will go off!); far away and it will be difficult to see any detail. To one side, you may get a strange view of things. Looking at it alone will be different from talking about it as you look at it with others, and your own state of mind will affect how you see it. Similarly, when we put the painting into a completely different frame, it will take on another form.

The purpose of reframing is to enable us to make a change in our life by considering other possibilities. It is easy to get stuck in one way of looking at a situation: reframing offers us new options and, as we know, in NLP the person with the most options controls the system.

There are several reasons why we might want to reframe a goal. Take 'weight loss' as an example. It is focusing on the very thing we don't want – 'weight'. How much more compelling it would be if we could focus on what we do want – a slim body, flat tum, size zero or whatever our goal really is. Secondly, it is an 'away from' goal because, again, it is what we *don't* want. The most important reason we need to reframe it is because it does not conform to any of the rules of SMART goals. It is totally **unspecific** – how much weight loss is going to mean success? One might go on and on for ever. It can be measured but which measure is the most meaningful: body fat ratio, waist or hip measurement, pounds or kilos lost? Who is to say what is achievable, what is realistic and in what context and when it is to be achieved by? Is it any wonder, then, that the weight loss business is so huge? Perhaps if we reframed weight loss, more people would succeed in being the size they want to be.

A SIX-STEP REFRAME TECHNIQUE

Bandler and Grinder developed their six-step reframe technique from work they did with Milton Erickson and Virginia Satir. Behind the process is the belief that every behaviour is useful in some way; it has a positive intention. Yes, even overeating!

- **Step 1** Identify the thing you want to change. In this example it is overeating.
- **Step 2** Establish communication with the part of you that overeats. Is it somewhere in your body or your mind? Is it an inner voice saying 'Go on, you deserve it, you've had a bad day' or a hungry feeling, the look of the dessert, the smell of chocolate?
- **Step 3** Consider what benefit it has for you. What positive thing is it trying to do for you? Does it want you to feel loved and full; have a nice sweet taste in your mouth; be one of the girls? Does it relieve your anxiety or boredom and make you feel good? Do you get out of doing something you don't want to do because you are overweight?
- **Step 4** Be curious. How could you satisfy that positive intention in a different way so that you could meet your outcome?
- **Step 5** Consider the options.
- **Step 6** Fast-forward and imagine yourself doing this new behaviour. Check that it will work. If it will, then you're done. If not, go back to Step 4 and come up with other options.

When considering your options, it can be helpful to ask yourself a few questions in order to understand the behaviour you're focusing on:

- How else could I view this behaviour?
- How might other people view it?
- In what context would this behaviour be appropriate?
- What's stopping me from changing my behaviour?

FIVE FRAMES

There are five ways of framing events:

The **outcome frame** is when we focus on the well-formed outcome, wording our goal as something we do want, and establishing it as a SMART goal – specific, measurable, achievable, realistic and timed. So in the context of weight loss we would instead decide on what weight or size we want to be by when and devise a plan to achieve it that we know is within our control. We can also visualize how we will look and feel when we are that weight. The reason some people don't succeed in losing weight is because they find it impossible to imagine themselves slim.

Dieting clubs use this outcome frame approach by setting goal weights at 5 or 10 per cent so there is always a goal within sight. They produce a plan based on 'points' or symbols such as traffic lights, weekly weigh-in meetings, recipes and sometimes a range of branded foods. They have watchwords like: 'See you slimmer next week.' Motivation is encouraged with stars and smiley-face stickers awarded and homework set to increase commitment.

The **backtrack frame** is where we go back to the first time we had the issue or behaviour we want to change and check whether this is behaviour we still want to pursue. Maybe it's no longer appropriate. We can continue patterns of behaviour without thinking. Maybe you started to eat more when you were at home with the kids or out of work, but have simply continued to do it despite the situation having changed.

The **evidence frame** is used to check on how you're doing – what evidence do you have that it's working? How do you feel? How do your clothes feel as you lose weight. How do you look? Keep checking how you're doing. When you have a lot of weight to lose, it's easy to feel downhearted, but check the evidence in the mirror. Respond to positive feedback. When people notice that you're losing weight, thank them and feel good about it rather than dismissing it.

The **'as if' frame** is where we behave as if we have already achieved our goal, so in this case we'd behave like a slim person, do what they do and eat what they eat. We can model people who are the size and shape we want to be and we would find that we ate less and were more active as a result. Acting 'as if' means that we do now what we'd planned to do once we lost weight, so apply for that new job, buy that new dress or take up tennis again.

The **ecology frame** is where you check how your outcome fits with those around you. Does your overeating fit with the people you spend time with? How can you keep your friends and family happy yet change your behaviour so you can meet your goal? Sometimes, couples get into habits and ways of eating and not exercising, but it can spiral out of control. One person then decides that they want to do something about it and lose weight but fears how their partner will react. They worry about being seen as disloyal in some way.

Putting it all together

Instead of having a weight-loss goal, reframe it by using the six-step reframe and identify the specific behaviour you want to change and the positive intention behind it, and come up with three alternative behaviours that will meet the same need and still achieve your desired outcome. Consider using one of the five different frames to help you reach your goal and overcome any barriers that might have stopped you in the past.

④ Understand the goal

9
10
11
12
13
14
15
16
17
18
19
20
21
22
23
24
25
26
27
28
29
30
31
32
33
34
35
36
37
38
39
40
41
42
43
44
45
46
47
48
49
50

 'The concept that the map is not the territory is one of the ideas that laid the foundations of Neuro Linguistic Programming. It means that your understanding of the world is based on how you represent it – your map – and not on the world itself.' Tony Robbins

 'Questions are also interventions. A good question can take a person's mind in a completely new direction and change his life. For example, ask yourself frequently, "What is the most useful question to ask now?"' John Seymour

 'Everybody is a genius. But if you judge a fish by its ability to climb a tree, it will live its whole life believing that it is stupid.' Albert Einstein

 'All experience is subjective.' Gregory Bateson

 'Put yourself in a state of mind where you say to yourself, "Here is an opportunity for you to celebrate like never before, my own power, my own ability to get myself to do whatever is necessary."' Tony Robbins

A goal is something we want, a state of mind such as confidence or calm, or it could be something more tangible such as a new job or to get married. How we frame it, or word it, will make a big difference to our chance of achieving it, but first we need to understand it and put it into a context. A good way to do this is by using the Logical Levels of Change, because this process causes us to align ourselves with our goal and in so doing address issues that enable us to understand it fully and the consequences for those around us.

Refer to the Logical Levels diagram in the Appendix. Your **purpose or goal** is at the top of the pyramid and you can answer the question for yourself about who you want to be. Remember to word it as a 'towards' goal because it can be tempting when we are in a problem state to think about what we *don't* want, such as not wanting to shout at the children, not wanting to miss a deadline, not wanting to be overweight, not wanting to smoke and so on. So think about what you do want and visualize yourself getting it – because when we can see, hear and feel ourselves having achieved our goal, there is far more chance of our succeeding at it.

Moving down a level, **who are you** when you're striving for this goal? For example, if your goal is to run a marathon, then your current identity would be 'training for the marathon' and this will define who you are right now and affect all the choices you make about eating healthily, keeping your fitness levels up, stretching and so on.

What **beliefs and values** do you have that underpin who you are as you head for this goal? You'll have lots of them but some will be particularly useful at this time, others less so. It might help to list the things that you believe relate to your goal, even putting them in order of importance. Your values will be those things that you hold to be important in life and they, too, should be aligned to your goal. If your goal is to get a promotion, this would be underpinned by the belief that you have the right experience for the job and that it would be a good career move. Your underlying value would be that it is important to progress in your career.

The next level, **skills and capabilities**, requires you to compile a list of all those things you do well that will enable you to achieve your goal. They may not be skills that directly relate to it, although many will, of course, but they may be skills that you have developed in other areas of your life that you can transfer to this one particular goal. These would be skills such as perseverance or courage, stamina, sense of humour and so on.

They would also include very specific skills such as being able to run, cook, write or speak a foreign language.

At the **behaviour** level, we focus on what we actually do in terms of our day-to-day behaviour and how we can change that in order to achieve our goal. In the marathon example, we might want to incorporate some training into our day a few times a week. What can you do now to change your behaviour?

Environment relates to where you live and work, with whom and how you can make changes to align yourself to your goal. You may have to change job, change the hours you work, move house or change something more minor to enable you to reach your goal.

UNDERSTANDING YOUR FITNESS GOAL.

Lots of us want to be fitter. We know that we are likely to live well into our 80s or even 90s, so we want to take care of our body so we have the best chance of an active old age. But what exactly does that mean?

We don't necessarily want to run marathons; indeed, we may not even want to run at all. Perhaps walking would form part of our fitness goal. If that is the case, we need to decide what sort of walking. There is power-walking, walking the dog, rambling, walking to work instead of taking the bus, walking upstairs instead of using the escalators or the lift. The more precise we can be in our planning, the more chance of we have of succeeding in achieving our end goal.

We need to decide what form our fitness will take: whether we are going to walk, run, swim, or play a sport and what type of exercise we want to include in our fitness regime. We also need to decide at what level we want to start, how we plan to progress and what level will satisfy us as having met our goal of being fit. This may be about frequency and duration, so think about for how long and how often you want to do a fitness activity. Whom will you do it with? Some of us are much better doing things in company rather than on our own, so know who you are and what is going to work for you.

UNDERSTANDING YOUR WEIGHT-LOSS GOAL

We want to lose weight, but this is an 'away from' goal, so understand your goal by thinking about what will constitute success. Will it be getting into that red leather jacket you bought in the sales or feeling lighter on your feet when you exercise, being able to see your feet or perhaps hearing others comment on how good you look. What do you want to see, hear or feel? Being able to imagine success is half the story and having the desire to achieve it is the motivation to construct a strategy that will work. Everyone will have a slightly different strategy, so knowing how yours will work and being prepared to constantly fine-tune it will ensure that you stay on track.

Also, think about your underlying values and beliefs. Why do you want this goal? Is it because you think it will make you happy? It may do but not if there are other things in your life that make you sad. Your weight is unlikely to be the sole reason you're unhappy, so losing weight alone won't change anything. Many people lack confidence in themselves and don't even like themselves very much. They then overeat as a comfort, but until you like yourself on the inside, changing the outside won't work. Instead, it may be more effective to make loving yourself your goal and get aligned by changing those things that contribute to your low self-esteem and the eating may well change as a result.

One of the problems with weight loss is that, if you have an identity of being 'a fat person', then it will be hard to change how you eat because fat people eat differently from thin people. Look at your identity and change it to align with your goal.

Some people don't even believe they can lose weight even when they are on a diet. What you believe will dictate what you achieve. Think about things you can do and what belief you have about that and you will realize that you need to change the weight-loss belief in line with it.

UNDERSTAND YOUR PARENTING GOAL

As parents, we want the best for our children and we hold ourselves responsible for bringing them up in a way that will help them grow into adults we can be proud of. However, we can get caught up in the minutiae of everyday life and we only notice everything they do wrong. Instead of having goals such as tidy bedrooms, homework done, sitting nicely at the table, eating their greens and so on, think instead about your underlying goal. When we constantly tell our children off, correct them and comment on what they could do better, our voice tends to rise, and we might even shout, and after a while children zone out because our voice becomes like wallpaper – just there.

Instead, take a goal that is bigger or more fundamental, something you truly believe is important. If, for example, it is to get them to do what they are told, make sure that, when you speak to them, you focus on that aspect and keep it consistent. It is easier for children to follow one instruction than lots of different ones. Also, when you observe them doing what they are told, you can point it out so they know when they are on track. By giving them positive attention for doing what they are told or taking responsibility or whatever you have decided is the big goal, and ignoring some of the minor transgressions, you will encourage them and motivate them to achieve it.

Putting it all together

In order to understand your goal, you need to give it context, understand what beliefs and values underpin it and then make the necessary changes at the different Logical Levels of Change in order to achieve it.

5 Understand other people's reactions

> 'There are persons who, when they cease to shock us, cease to interest us.' F.H. Bradley

> 'Breast milk, semen, sweat, tears, and mucus are not created freely when we are super reasonable... the juices are drying out.' Virginia Satir

> 'We must not allow other people's limited perceptions to define us.' Virginia Satir

> 'The meeting of two personalities is like the contact of two chemical substances: if there is any reaction, both are transformed.' Carl Jung

> 'Dreams have only one owner at a time. That's why dreamers are lonely.' Erma Bombeck

When we make changes in our life, achieve successes or experience setbacks, the people around us react. Sometimes they will say something so you'll get a verbal reaction, and other times you'll be able to read it in their body language. Either way, they are communicating. Virginia Satir, who was a significant model for Bandler and Grinder as they developed NLP, described four survival stances or ways of being and a fifth, congruent stance. They are, in effect, ways of coping and you will observe these in others' response to you. Here's how to recognize them.

Placating is when someone disregards their own feelings and hands over power to the other person. They want to please them, not just in the way people generally want to be pleasant but more as a matter of course because they don't believe their opinion matters. So, even if they didn't feel very good about what you've done, they will still be full of praise (through clenched teeth). You might experience this at a weight-loss meeting when you've done really well and they haven't – they will nevertheless make a big fuss and tell you how amazing you are. Their needs are not important. Placaters can often be identified by the phrase 'I'm sorry', as they go about apologizing for things they aren't even responsible for. So, if you have a setback, they will say, 'I'm so sorry.' They sometimes have high whiny voices.

The opposite of placating is **blaming** and you'll get this reaction from some people who think whatever has happened is all your fault, because it certainly isn't theirs. They can be abusive and violent at worst and at best nagging, judgemental and fault-finding.

Being **super reasonable** is another type of response and you'll experience people being very sensible and logical. It is usually accompanied by a rigid body posture and an expressionless face. They will be objective and avoid talk of feelings, keeping a monotonous tone to their voice. In order to appear detached, they will use long words and wordy sentences, not bothering whether you understand what they're saying.

Distracting is the fourth response, where someone behaves in a silly, clownish way. It is the opposite of the super-reasonable stance. People do this to avoid confronting the issue and to take attention away from it. They are the joker in the group and people enjoy their company, but they are not sincere and can change tack, interrupt and hold conflicting views all at the same time, and are not in alignment.

WHO'S WHO?

Once you have identified these 'survival stances', as Satir names them, you might want to think about the people around you and categorize them. If you are looking for support for a difficult and somewhat emotional decision, and feel you need someone who can be objective, then the computer nature of the super-reasonable friend is what you would seek out.

If you're looking for someone to distract you out of a grumpy mood or a bit of depression, then the clowning of the distracter will be just what you need.

It's hard to think that you would have any need for the blamer in your life, but you might need a placater occasionally if you just want someone to comfort you and take away those negative feelings.

HOW DO YOU COPE WITH OTHER PEOPLE'S NEGATIVE REACTIONS?

Recognize that these emotions belong to them and not you. Check in with your own emotions and ask yourself how you are feeling about the situation. You can't take responsibility for their emotions. Remind yourself what you think and feel.

Give them some feedback. Remember to be positive first, then say what you'd like more or less of and finally finish on a positive note.

Separate yourself mentally by tuning out if you can't separate yourself physically. Let their comments wash over you. You could use a calming anchor to help with this. If this type of situation happens a lot, give yourself a zoning-out anchor and use it. You might enjoy a nice visual anchor of a beach somewhere hot and sunny or an auditory anchor of some music you can play in your head or a word you can use to stay calm. A kinaesthetic anchor may be to tap your finger on your knee under the table. Use the time constructively to plan something or work on something that you have to do.

Breathe. Changing your physiology is the fastest way to change your state, so change your breathing by taking deep breaths. Look up and to the right to visualize the end of the situation and how it will feel, look and sound.

EXTERNALLY VS. INTERNALLY REFERENCED

Just how concerned should you be with other people's reactions to you and what you say, think and do?

Imagine a sliding scale. At one end is the state of being totally **externally** referenced, where you have no opinion yourself but are completely governed by everyone else's reactions and feelings. You ask people what they think and take on that stance, but then when you meet someone else and discuss it with them you take on their view as your own. When anything happens you reserve judgement on whether you should be pleased or not until you've checked it out with your friends or colleagues.

At the other end of the scale is being totally **internally** referenced. This means that you check out with your own values and beliefs and this is more important than anyone else's view. You say and do what you think you should do with no regard for anyone else.

So where do you need to be along this scale? It may well depend on the situation. Everything you do is going to affect other people – 'no man is an island'. Some decisions require more inner reflection than others, and only you know who is involved and how important they need to be in the decision-making. The important factor is to be aware of the scale and where you are on it at any point, so that, if you fear that you may be a little more externally referenced than you need to be, or a little more internally referenced, you can slide along and either check in with others or with yourself.

Putting it all together

Other people's reactions are just that – theirs. Depending on the nature of the situation, you can decide how much attention to give them. You can also use the Satir stances described at the start of this chapter to understand what is underlying their reactions.

6) Know whom to model

'When we step into someone else's shoes and reproduce what they do and the results they achieve, we are modelling.' Sue Knight

'In modelling we elicit the strategies, beliefs, values and fundamental filters and the physiology that allows someone to produce certain behaviour. Then we codify these in a series of steps designed to make the behaviour easy to reproduce.' Jeremy Lazarus

'What are the behavioural patterns of successful people? How do they achieve their results? What do they do that is different from people who are not successful? What is the difference that makes the difference? The answers to these questions have generated all the skills, techniques and presuppositions associated with NLP.' Joseph O'Connor

'The purpose of modelling is to identify 'what is' and how 'what is' works without influencing what is being modelled. The modeller begins with an open mind, a blank sheet and an outcome to discover the way a system functions without attempting to change it.' James Lawley and Penny Tompkins

'Imagine being able to have any skill you want and learning it quickly and easily without having to slog away for years or waste time by trial and error? It has been demonstrated time and time again that once you understand the thinking patterns and behaviours used by the most brilliant and talented in any field, you can learn to do what they can do.'
Steve Bavister and Amanda Vickers

Modelling in NLP is the process by which we can acquire new skills. It is based on the understanding that, if we find someone who has the skill we want, then by copying its structure and the underlying belief, we can have it for ourselves. It is a very powerful technique enabling us to incorporate into ourselves other people's skills and gifts. The excellence that we model is something we think someone does better than anyone else but we, too, can have our own excellence. We have skills we use in another part of our life that we want to transfer – that, too, can be modelled.

Imagine you are someone who procrastinates and that you have a writing assignment to complete by a certain deadline. In order to meet this deadline, you want to learn from someone who can focus and get the job done. So first you find a few people who can do this really well. You observe them and work out how they do this. What do they do first, then next, and so on? Notice what you see and hear and the actions you witness. If you were to go away and copy this structure, you may improve your result, but you won't get the same result as them because your thinking is different. You know your thinking is different because, if it were the same, you'd not get the result you get now. So you need to find out what they are thinking. You need to find out their values and beliefs about getting things done by the deadline. What's different in their thinking that leads to a 'get it done now' attitude rather than procrastinating?

You can get their thinking and underlying beliefs by asking them directly, 'What's important to you about getting things done?' and then go through the structure again with this answer and way of thinking in your mind. You can also think about your own life. Is there an area of your life where you don't in fact procrastinate and you are action oriented? We don't behave the same way in all situations. Perhaps in sport or at home or work there may be something you do with focus, determination and speed. Imagine you're doing that now. What's the underlying belief about why you're doing this like this? Take this belief and apply it to where you need it.

It is extremely important when modelling to select models who are not only excellent exemplars of the skill but also people who will be willing and able to explain their underlying beliefs and values. Many gifted and skilled people may be unable to get in touch with their feelings and, even less, express them in a way that you can understand and use. In order for us to replicate the model of excellence, we must take on their beliefs. It is much easier than you think to take on someone's belief and it starts by saying to yourself, 'What if I believed this?' and then acting 'as if' you do. Once we have their structure and beliefs, we can start thinking about the values they must have underpinning them. We test out our hypotheses by repeating what we have observed and taking on the beliefs and values. One by one, we remove different elements to find out which parts of our model are the ones we need to replicate the excellence. Then we have our model, which we can then teach to others – indeed, the proof of how successfully we have modelled will lie in our ability to pass it on to others, who can then get the same result.

SPORTING LIFE

Do you want to model your sporting hero? If you play a sport, there will certainly be someone whose style you will want to emulate. You probably watch them already, try to copy their swing, their moves, yet somehow you just don't get the same result. The chances are that you may not be focusing on every part of the move. The structure will be how everything works together from before the beginning of the move to after the end. Watch them more closely right the way through and, if possible, watch it in slow motion. You may be focusing your attention on the arm if you're watching a swing or a serve in tennis, but each time you watch the same action focus on a different part of the body so you get the whole structure. A good person to model would be someone you can do this with. It needs to be someone who consistently gets the result you want.

The next part of the process is to find out the underlying belief. It's quite easy with sporting heroes to get this from interviews, autobiographies and articles in the newspaper, where sportsmen and sportswomen are specifically asked about what they are thinking at different moments in the game. In this sense, celebrity models work better than others because not only are their thoughts better documented but they also have better access to them than 'normal' people, who, while they may make a lot of great shots, will not be so consistent and may not be so aware of their thinking process.

HEALTHY BELIEFS

Many people use models of excellence in order to combat ill health. They find people or are put in touch with people, via the hospital or the doctor, who have recovered from the illness. They can then talk with them about how they did it, about their diet, exercise regime, medicine or alternative treatments. They can also talk with them about their beliefs and values. Recovery from illness takes strong beliefs, and it can be difficult at times to retain such beliefs when the evidence may be suggesting that they are not working.

We are all different and so are our illnesses and disabilities. However, there is evidence to suggest that it is the belief that we hold that makes the difference in how we cope with them and to what degree they limit us. Two people with similar disabilities can be completely different: one person may use their disability to avoid doing things and says 'I can't…' whereas another person with an 'I can…' belief will find ways to get it done.

You need to find people to model whose belief is what you feel you need to get yourself through the illness or disability you have.

CHILDREN AND MODELLING

Children enjoy modelling their TV and video-game heroes. When they have problems with fears and anxieties, asking them to imagine they are their hero works very well in getting them into a brave state of mind where they can conquer their fears. Ask 'What would X do?' Children have fantastic imaginations and can easily turn into their hero and take on their persona in order to feel brave. This is a much better strategy than crawling around under the bed talking to imaginary monsters.

If they want to be better at schoolwork, they can emulate the person in their class who gets the best marks. They need to find out how this child succeeds; what is his or her strategy? Does he or she learn visually, auditorially or kinaesthetically? What is his or her process? When does the process start? It may start much earlier than when he or she starts the work.

Find out the child's beliefs by asking, 'How do you do it?' If the child is quite young, you could perhaps ask his or her parents. It's also helpful to know why it is important for him or her to do it well. Some children achieve because they want to do well and others because they don't want to fail or do badly. Which strategy does that child use and which does your child use? Generally, a 'towards strategy' works better than an 'away from' one.

Putting it all together

You can choose exemplars or models of excellence by being curious as you watch people whose performance in your chosen field is excellent. You will need many exemplars because it may take a few attempts to find the exact part of their model that you need for your strategy. It is tempting to want to take their whole strategy, but you need only the part that will make the difference between success and failure to your own strategy. It is essential to observe, copy, test, tweak and repeat until you consistently get the result you want and can pass it on to someone else as a model of success.

7 Keep the goal within control

'You want what you want, whether or not you think you can get it.' Robert Fritz

'Put yourself in a state of mind where you say to yourself, "Here is an opportunity for you to celebrate like never before, my own power, my own ability to get myself to do whatever is necessary."' Tony Robbins

'Science, like art, religion, commerce, warfare, and even sleep, is based on presuppositions.' Gregory Bateson

'The greatest personal limitation is to be found not in the things you want to do and can't, but in the things you've never considered doing.' Richard Bandler

'It all depends on how we look at things, and not on how they are themselves.' Carl Jung

When goal-setting, we are frequently cautioned to set a goal that is within our control. Yet, who is to say what is in our control? Anything that involves other people will not normally be within our control because we have no control over others. Anything that requires scientific or technological advances not currently available will also be out of our control. However, there remain a great number of areas that, while appearing to be out of our control, can actually be managed by using NLP.

When we talk about a goal being within our control, we mean that it is not dependent on the actions of others. So, for example, we could have a goal for our marriage to last 50 years but we cannot control our partner's feelings, health or actions. Similarly, we might have a goal of getting that great job, but we cannot control who else will be going for it, how they perform at interview, their qualifications and who the interviewer will select on the day. Goals need to focus on what we can control ourselves, so these goals need to be reworded accordingly. You can, however, use NLP techniques to build rapport in your marriage and in your job interview as well as everywhere else in life. Do this by matching other people's body language and language patterns.

It is important to be aware of what we can control but not lose sight of those things that we have more control over than we think. For example, many people feel that they can't control their health, but there is lots of evidence that we can control it using NLP. People who think positively will always be healthier than those who don't. There are regularly examples of people who have freed themselves of cancer through these means. Believing that you have control gives you a strong mental attitude for fighting disease and physical disability. It is said that if the Paralympic athletes were able-bodied they would outperform any able-bodied athlete because of their superior mental control.

Remember, if one person has done it then you can, when you model it. The essential ingredient is to have the belief that you can do it when you have the structure of their excellence. This you can control.

DOING 'THE IMPOSSIBLE'

Until it was discovered that the world was a sphere and not flat, it was believed that it was impossible to travel round the world. The idea that humans could fly was thought impossible and many people who have been paralysed can now walk.

When we talk about keeping our goals within our control, we don't mean setting goals that we can achieve now. We mean that you should set goals that are possible because someone somewhere can do it and therefore you can model them.

Modelling in NLP terms means that you find examples of excellence, people who have done what you want to do. Someone somewhere will have done it and, if they can, then you can too.

The way you can model them is to initially do what they have done, copying exactly the structure of it. Watch how they do what they do, listen to what they say, ask them about their inner voice, and do what they do.

But this isn't enough. The reason they are able to do what you want to do is because they believe something that currently you don't believe. Find out about their beliefs. The difference that makes the difference in achieving your goal will be the belief in the possibility of so doing.

How do you find out their beliefs? Ask them: 'What do you believe about doing this thing?' You'll find out the beliefs and values they have that make it possible to achieve it. You need to take on that belief if you are to be successful too. The way we do this is to imagine having the belief. Act 'as if' you already have that belief in your everyday life first and then try it out with all the actions, thoughts and inner voice of your model.

USE THE SECOND POSITION

There are three ways, or positions, in which to look at any situation. We will have more control in most situations when we use the second position.

First position is us and how we are thinking at that moment. It is simply our own perception based on our memories, experiences, values and beliefs.

Second position is the other person and their view of the world. When we understand how their values and beliefs will shape their actions, we gain more control of the situation. We do this by being curious about them, noticing what they do in different environments, listening for their values and beliefs and learning about their past experiences that shape how they are today.

Sports coaches will study the past form of teams they're playing against, the players and how different venues may affect them.

By knowing your opponent you can control to some extent the outcome of the match because it will inform how you perform. While we may be playing in a team or playing against an opponent whom we can't control, there are ways of playing that will control how the ball will land and therefore control how the opponent will play it back.

In an interview situation, by studying articles about the company and finding out as much as you can about the person who will be interviewing you, it is possible to increase rapport and choose relevant topics and experience to refer to in the interview that will impress and interest them.

CONTROLLING THE UNCONTROLLABLE

Many people think you can't control relationships or rapport and that it is all a matter of chemistry and whether you 'click' or 'gel'. Whether you get a date actually is determined before you even step out of your front door: How you dress, your state of mind and your beliefs about the possibility of getting a date are determined way in advance. If you start getting ready for your date thinking that they won't be attracted to you, that they might not even turn up, that you won't have anything in common, that they won't want to see you again, then this will be your reality. It will permeate your state, your choice of clothes, conversation and your body language. Your date will pick this up and decide along the lines you've determined yourself. If, instead, you get ready thinking what a fun evening you'll have, how you can't wait to meet them and find out about them, you're already thinking of things to talk about and you are dressing to impress them, your date is much more likely to turn out the way you want it to.

When we meet people, there are ways we can achieve our goal of getting on with them even though we can't directly influence them to do or say what we want. We do this with rapport building. First, notice how they are standing or sitting and copy it. We get on best when we are at the same eye level and appear to be in a similar pose, so whatever they are doing, do it too.

Secondly, listen for their language patterns. Is the other person using images as they speak, are they carefully choosing their words or are they fidgeting a lot and gesturing? Match their language patterns and they will feel that you are both talking the same language. People do business with people like them and people they like, so focus on them rather than what you have to say.

Thirdly, give them good eye contact, pay attention to them and be curious about them. You will build good rapport when they believe you are paying attention to what they have to say and are not regarding your mobile or looking around the room. Nod and shake your head to show you are on board. Repeat the last few words with a questioning intonation to encourage them to continue.

When you have good rapport, you can start introducing your own agenda using their language patterns and body language, and you will find that they will follow your lead as you originally followed theirs. You can indicate this change of leadership with a pause, a change in breathing pattern, or a movement such as switching to leaning forward or by uncrossing or crossing your legs.

Putting it all together

By establishing rapport, being curious about the other person and by modelling excellence, we can acquire control of our own goal when it might previously have seemed out of our control. If one person has achieved it, then you can too. Remember, though, that the first person who achieved it had no one to model, but they believed so strongly and passionately in the goal that they made it happen for themselves. How much do you want this goal?

8 Use metaphors to gain confidence

CC *'Metaphors can be enchanting, enticing and mesmerising. Their effects may be enlightening and empowering when they are developed and recounted constructively.'* Sue Knight

'Stories get to the parts that other words don't reach. They speak to you at an unconscious level. They enable you to convey information indirectly, to pace someone's current reality and then lead them on to a new one. To move away from problems to different outcomes. To open up new possibilities.'
Romilla Ready and Kate Burton

CC *'Metaphors are not simply poetic or rhetorical embellishments, but powerful devices for shaping perception and experience.'*
Nick Owen

CC *'Metaphors illuminate some aspects of an experience while leaving others aspects in the shadows.'* James Lawley and
Penny Tompkins

'All which is not concrete is metaphoric – clearly, this involves the vast majority of our everyday experiences. The structure of the unconscious – easily the most influential factor in our success in life – or more correctly said, the relationship which we have with our unconscious is easily the most important factor in our success in life – is that of metaphor.' John Grinder

CC *'The unconscious contains no nouns, only verbs – the part of language which carries the representation of the relationships*

and processes which determine the quality of our lives. This in part accounts for the fact that the typical production of the unconscious is metaphoric: dreams, poems, dances, songs and stories.' John Grinder

In NLP, we use the term 'metaphor' to describe analogies, jokes, parables and stories, similes and allegories. It is an indirect way of communicating that bypasses the conscious mind and, used creatively and appropriately, it can have more of an impact than direct speech because we conjure up images and mental pictures rather than being restricted simply by the meaning of the word. The metaphor speaks of our relationship to the word. We use metaphors in everyday life when we express something in terms of something else – for example 'Life is like a bed of roses' or 'Mealtimes can be like a battle zone.' It is a good way to communicate a lot of complex information very efficiently, disclosing far more than we would have had we used just a literal description. We can use metaphors to understand our feelings and create new metaphors for more resourceful ones.

We each have a preferred way to process our world – visual, auditory or kinaesthetic – although we will use all three at various times. For each of these, there are two ways we use them, literally and metaphorically, so if you are kinaesthetic you will use action and feeling words but also symbols and metaphors that are likely to also be physical e.g. 'a lump in my throat' or 'a step too far.' Most of the time we are unaware of our subconscious metaphors until someone asks us 'what's that like?' and we access it, although it was there in our head all the time.

What typifies a metaphor is the word 'like'. We look for patterns in our life. We ask: 'So this experience is like what other experience?' When we encounter new things, we search our memory for something similar we do know about that will enable us to make sense of the new experience. Our brain naturally looks for patterns and it enables us to form links and learn new skills as we transfer them from one situation to another. Our unconscious mind, by creating a metaphor, creates new meanings and solves problems by distracting us from the content and engaging us in process.

The metaphor could be **direct**, where there is an obvious link between one situation and another – for example comparing learning a new software program with learning a foreign language, in that both involve learning. Or it can be **indirect**, where the link is less obvious, so comparing learning the new software program with planning a dinner-party menu. In that instance, we are invited to use our imagination to figure out what the similarities might be and we can explore this with the other person to discover how they are similar in their mind. We often see brand logos and advertising campaigns using metaphor powerfully to create unconscious connections in people's minds without actually spelling them out.

If we apply this process to our lack of confidence, for example, we need first to identify situations in which we lack confidence. It was like what? You might find it easier to think of your metaphor if you associate into the experience, so close your eyes and imagine you are in this situation where you lack confidence right now. Picture what you see, notice who is there and what you hear and feel. Then, when it is quite intense, ask yourself, 'What is this like?', 'What is it similar to?'

In their work on clean language and metaphors, Penny Tompkins and James Lawleyr found that most metaphors fell into these categories. Use the list as a prompt if you need to.

- The human body (including health and illness)
- Living things (animals and plants)
- People-made things (buildings, machines, tools)
- Human activities (games, cooking, food, sport, war)
- The environment (heat, cold, light, dark)
- Physics (space, forces, movement, direction)

Indeed, even talking about 'building confidence' uses a metaphor. If you think of building confidence, then how do you build it? Do you construct it a brick at a time? Where do you start? What do you make it from? What is your metaphor for confidence? Confidence is like what? If it was an object, what would it be? Does it have a colour? How big is it? Where is it situated? How close is it to you? We can use submodalities to make our confidence more accessible by imagining it smaller, more accessible and closer to us. When asking yourself or helping someone else identify and explore their metaphor, use clean questions to avoid making any assumptions about the other person's metaphor or limiting your own choices.

12 BASIC CLEAN LANGUAGE QUESTIONS

Developing questions

- And is there anything else about (that) [x]?
- And what kind of [x] (is that [x])?
- And where/whereabouts is [x]?
- And that [x] is like what?
- And is there a relationship between [x] and [y]?
- And when [x], what happens to [y]?

Moving time questions

- And what happens just before [event x]?
- And then what happens? / And what happens next?
- And where could/does [x] come from?

Intention questions

- And what would you/[x] like to have happen?
- And what needs to happen for [x] to [intention of x]?
- And can [x] [intention of x]?

LET'S PLAY WITH METAPHORS

Here are some situations you may sometimes encounter. Think about how you would complete each sentence. You can choose an object or another activity, so 'Giving a dinner party is like climbing the Eiffel Tower'. Why? Because it's exhausting, pretty exciting once it's done, and a slightly foreign and unfamiliar task, albeit enjoyable. Or 'Giving a dinner party is like a battle.' Why? Because it's messy and takes a long time and you don't get the credit for all the effort.

- Giving a presentation is like…
- Asking my boss for a day off is like…
- Finding a birthday present for my partner is like…
- Speaking a foreign language is like…
- Giving birth is like…

- Going to the gym is like…
- Being in debt is like…
- Making decisions is like…

Now think up some of your own…

Notice how your metaphor may be contributing to how you feel about the subject matter. How would your attitudes and feelings change if you switched the metaphor for one that will be more effective?

FROM UNRESOURCEFUL TO RESOURCEFUL METAPHORS

Having explored the existing metaphor and understood how it is working in an unresourceful way, we need now to replace it with a resourceful one. Think about how you'd like to be in the situation you have been working on. How confident do you want to be? Confident like what?

If you are helping a child or teenager access an engaging metaphor for confidence, you could ask them to think of a celebrity or TV character, book character or video-game hero who captures this confidence for them. Younger children enjoy using animal metaphors. So: 'What animal are you when you're scared?' and 'What animal would you like to be instead?'

You may also want to conjure up a historical figure, TV personality or similar as your metaphor for confidence, although these are more models of excellence than metaphors.

Your metaphor might be your own model of excellence, so you may want to be 'confident in public speaking like you are confident in singing' or confident at cooking as you are confident in writing.

Your metaphor for being confident may have visual elements such as appearance – 'like a princess', 'like a teenager' – or auditory aspects such as quality of sound or volume – 'clear as a bell', 'like a foghorn', or be characterized by action or speed – 'like a bat out of hell', 'like a shot'.

Once you have your metaphor, use a **circle of excellence** to anchor it. Imagine a circle on the floor in front of you and stand in it as you imagine yourself having the confidence of this metaphor. Bring it into the present and imagine yourself doing the thing you want to do like the metaphor you have brought to mind. When the image fades, step out and then repeat the process a few times until you get the state of confidence whenever you step into it.

Use this whenever you need to and be the metaphor you have created.

Putting it all together

Metaphors are a very creative way to use our imagination to take ourselves into a more resourceful state where we feel confident. We can use a metaphor that is directly linked to being confident but using another situation, or one that is indirectly linked where we associate confidence with something different – an object, an activity or a living thing. Use clean questions to elicit the detail and understanding of the metaphor and find a resourceful one to replace ones that are not working for you, then anchor it using a circle of excellence.

9 Focus on what you want

> 'In order to say no to something, your brain must first make an image of the thing you don't want and then negate it. The problem is that at this point you're already heading in the wrong direction.' Richard Bandler

> 'If you don't know where you're going, you will probably end up somewhere else.' Lawrence J. Peter

> 'Believe you can and you're halfway there.' Theodore Roosevelt

> 'If you can dream it you can do it.' Walt Disney

> 'The secret of getting ahead is getting started.' Mark Twain

Have you heard the expression 'Don't think about pink elephants!'? What do we find ourselves doing? Thinking about pink elephants, of course. In order to make sense of the instruction, we first have to get a picture in our head of a pink elephant. So we have now done exactly what we have been told not to do, even though it wasn't our intention. That's how negative goals work, too. As we focus on what we don't want, inadvertently we are actually getting it.

Thinking about what you don't want is **problem thinking,** whereas thinking about what you do want is **outcome thinking**. Problem thinking arises when we focus on the thing that's happening now, which is of course the thing we don't want. So the only way we will change and experience more of what we do want is to move away from the present problem state and towards the compelling outcome.

There are two directions in life, forwards and backwards, towards and away from. When Bandler and Grinder developed NLP back in the 1960s they found that successful people were all 'towards'-oriented. They didn't waste their time and energy on what they didn't want but focused on getting what they did want.

'Away from' thinking focuses the mind on the present unsatisfactory situation that they want to change. When we try to get our brain to focus on what it doesn't want, it gets confused. Think about some of these goals; have you ever had goals like these?

'I want to give up smoking.'

'I must get rid of all the junk in this room.'

'I've got to lose weight.'

'I don't want to come last.'

'I hope I don't fail.'

'I'd better not catch his cold.'

'I don't want to be late.'

Have you ever told yourself 'I mustn't forget to…' and then found that you did indeed forget whatever it was. Your brain is saying, 'Forget…' whereas, if instead you told yourself 'Remember to…', you'd have a lot more chance of being successful. On leaving the house for work, my husband often tells me 'Don't forget to…' and consciously I have to reword it 'I must remember…', otherwise I know I'll forget. It happens sometimes with children, doesn't it? You say, 'Be careful not to fall!' and then they do just that. It's because subconsciously they've heard the instruction to fall and they've focused on that word.

When people are focusing on the problem and being in a problem state, there can be fear about what they'll do when the problem's fixed. What will they focus on next? Will there be a void in their life? Some people worry that they won't know what to do with themselves when they are no longer worrying about this thing. This is another very good reason for focusing on something enjoyable, something they do want or who they want to be.

TRYING TIMES

The word 'try' is the enemy of successful goal-setting. It is simply a variation on problem-state thinking. How many times do you hear people state their goal in this way: 'I'm trying to lose weight' or 'I'm trying to leave my boring job' or 'I'm trying to stop shouting at the kids'?

The word 'trying' implies that you doubt whether you'll be successful but nevertheless you're going to put it out there as a goal. However, by using the word 'try' no one is convinced you mean it, so you won't get any support. How hard are you trying, really? It sounds as if this is a goal that you think you ought to have because someone else has suggested it, or you have read a book or magazine article that recommends it, so you're going to give it a 'try'.

Instead, remove the word 'try' and replace it with the belief that it is important. It is something you do want to do, so start picturing how success would look. If, when you do this, it isn't that compelling, then change your goal to one that is.

Trying does not form any part of goal-setting and doesn't belong there. Instead, word your goal in the positive as something that you will be or get and take responsibility for achieving it.

'I WANT…'

As part of your personal development, start thinking about what you do want in every situation.

Even, for example, when you're shopping and you're looking for a parking space, think in terms of 'I want a parking space' rather than 'I bet I won't get a parking space.' Amazingly, it has been proved that people are more likely to get what they desire (yes, even parking spaces) when they focus positive energy on what they want.

It may seem obvious to focus on what you want but the meaning of the communication is the response it elicits. I recently had a client who told me that every night her daughter comes in and wakes her up several times. 'I tell her every night, "Do not disturb me during the night'', she told me, 'and yet she does it again. I don't know what to do.' She has told her daughter not to come in, not to wake her up or disturb her, but she hasn't told her what she does want instead. It would be much clearer and more effective to tell her daughter to stay in her room until the morning.

It's not just about what we say and how we think, it's the way we live our life and what we notice. When we notice what's going well – the good decisions and choices we are making and the steps we are taking along the road to our goal – rather than pouncing on the disappointments and false moves, we will find ourselves closer to our goal.

'WHEN…HOW…WHERE'

Apart from wording your goal in the positive as something you *do* want, you can also orient yourself towards getting it by adding in words like 'when', for example. 'When I am fit, I will…' or 'When I have passed my exam, I will…' Add to this by building a picture of how you will look and where you will be. Can you get an image in your mind of yourself in the future?

People who are able to picture themselves as a leader, manager and powerful influencer within their organization start working towards this role by dressing the part, networking and impressing those they need to impress. They not only want to see themselves in the role but they also want others to picture them there.

When you talk about that time in the future when you will have achieved your goal, you make it start happening by taking on a different identity. Someone wanting to become healthier eats and behaves differently from someone who has a goal of 'trying not to eat the wrong sort of food', and people wanting to move up the career ladder make sure that their work is done to deadline and that they behave in a way that shows them in the best possible light.

When you talk about your goal like this and take on the new identity, it starts to become your reality. Your future is already becoming your present. There is no question in your mind that you will achieve your goal, as using the words 'If I get fit,

I will…' would suggest. When we think in terms of 'If I achieve my goal…', it suggests that there is some doubt in your mind that it may not happen. It also firmly places you in today's problem state as opposed to being on the way to a future where your goal has been met.

Putting it all together

Focusing on what we do want rather than on what we don't want is a matter of thinking first what we really want, imagining what it will be like and taking it on as our identity. This moves us from a state of problem thinking, where the focus is on what we don't want, and moves us along the road towards what we do want – which is our compelling vision for ourselves.

10 Know who you are when the goal is achieved

 'Success is not final, failure is not fatal: it is the courage to continue that counts.' Winston Churchill

 'Think twice before you speak, because your words and influence will plant the seed of either success or failure in the mind of another.' Napoleon Hill

'Be a yardstick of quality. Some people aren't used to an environment where excellence is expected.' Steve Jobs

'A man who wants to lead the orchestra must turn his back on the crowd.' Max Lucado

 'Free your expectation of the future from the grip of past failure.' John Seymour

So we set a goal and we work towards it with passion and commitment, applying all our skills, and eventually we succeed, but who are we now? How do we decide that we've truly reached our goal, and is there another one to go for? We will have changed through reaching this milestone, so how can we prepare ourselves for it? There are a lot of questions here, so let's consider our new identity and how we will equip ourselves to live with it.

Using the Logical Levels diagram in the Appendix, we can align ourselves with our goal in all parts of our life. Goals frequently slip out of reach when we aim for something but do it in the same environment, with the same skills, behaviours and beliefs.

When we achieve a goal we have a new identity that needs to be in alignment with our new behaviour, beliefs and skills.

Look forward to when you have achieved your goal – who are you now and what is your mission? What are the beliefs and values you have now and how do they affect you – now and in the future? As someone who has achieved this goal, you presumably believed it was important and had value to you and who you are and want to be. You need to sustain these values and the skills you have acquired along the way. Your behaviour has enabled you to meet the goal and this needs to continue if you are to support it. For example, if your goal was to lose weight, you will have needed to change your behaviour to succeed, but if that stops now that you have achieved the weight loss, you will simply return to the weight you were in no time. This is why so often diets don't work – people go back to their old behaviour.

Your environment will have changed, too, perhaps in order to support the goal, so keep that in place to sustain it. For example, if your goal was to achieve a certain handicap in golf, you will have had to practise (behaviour), up your game with some lessons from a pro (skills), exchange tips with other golfers (environment) and believe that it is possible (belief) and of value to you. Once you have achieved this handicap, if you then stopped playing (to take an absurd example), your handicap would soon go down.

If you'd like to have a technique to remind you of the new identity that you are aiming for as a way to keep you on track, how about using an anchor? Anchor the feeling of being focused and determined to achieve your goal. A good technique here is to use the **circle of excellence**. Imagine a circle on the floor in front of you. As you think about your new identity and how much you want to have it, step into that circle and imagine you have it now. Visualize yourself in the new identity, notice what you see, hear and feel in the new identity, and give it all the rich tones of the here and now as if you have it right now. When it fades, step out of the circle and give yourself a little shake. Then repeat it. Whenever you need to experience it, you know you just need to step forward into that circle of excellence.

1
2
3
4
5
6
7
8
9
(10)
11
12
13
14
15
16
17
18
19
20
21
22
23
24
25
26
27
28
29
30
31
32
33
34
35
36
37
38
39
40
41
42
43
44
45
46
47
48
49
50

WORK GOAL

We are striving for a promotion and our boss has told us what they are looking for. We have to demonstrate certain skills and maybe reach sales targets or present strategies – whatever it is, we know what has to be done and how to do it. After a time, it will be decided that we will have that promotion, so we will be more senior, have more money and perhaps have people working under us. It will involve new responsibilities, travel perhaps and maybe a move. We put these things to one side, though, as we work towards our goal.

However, we need to start thinking about who we will be when we have reached our goal. What will our identity be and how will it sit with our values and beliefs? Are there aspects of your new role that will sit uncomfortably with you? How will you handle this? Perhaps there are arrangements that need to be made now or discussions you need to have, both with those you work with and those you live with.

How will other people relate to us when we have reached our goal? Are they competing with us and will they be resentful if we achieve it and they don't? Start thinking about how to manage their reactions, and how you can build rapport and form good working relationships with them now.

A promotion at work will bring with it a change in identity and a change in the dynamics between you and the people you work with now and those you will work with in the future, so think about what you want to change in order for these dynamics to work.

PERSONAL GOAL

Imagine you want to meet someone special, have a relationship and settle down. This is very different from being single and not in a relationship. How will you align yourself once this goal is achieved? You will need to make fundamental changes in your life to accommodate another person and their needs. How will you do this? What will you give up in order to make space for someone else? What changes and sacrifices will you be prepared to make? Think about what sort of relationship you want before you decide to commit, while you can still think rationally and before your life changes. What values do you hold about relationships and what beliefs do you have about what makes a relationship work?

Who will you be in the relationship? What will your identity be? Some married couples spend years working this out, only to find themselves incompatible, so instead think it through before you prepare to enter the relationship and live with these values and beliefs in place, rather than only recognizing them once they have been violated.

Big changes in identity at the personal level can take some adapting to, whether it be meeting and settling down with someone, starting a family, giving up work or moving. Instead of leaving these things to chance, decide now where you stand on the important issues and be clear about your identity when you've achieved your goal.

WEIGHT-LOSS GOAL

You know who you are now, overweight and on a diet, but who will you be when you have achieved your weight-loss goal? You will be slim and healthy. You will be proud of yourself for having achieved your goal. You will wear smaller clothes and people will look at you differently. Perhaps you will attract more attention; perhaps your partner will be jealous of the attention you will get. You may want to go out more, spend more money on clothes, keep up a fitness regime. Life will be different for you when you have achieved your goal. You will want to stay slim, so this will mean eating differently. You need to think about how this will affect your daily life, especially if you cook for the family. If you eat at work, you will need to choose food that maintains your trim figure and this may affect what you do if you usually eat in the canteen or with work colleagues.

We get very used to how we look and sometimes don't realize how we've put on weight until we look at old photos and realize. Similarly, when we lose it, we may feel the same inside but it's others who view us differently because we look different. We look slim.

There is often an expectation that fat people are jolly and that's often a persona we're happy to take on to mask how we feel about ourselves. But what about when we are slim? How will we be then? Will we still be the jolly person in the group? What role in your group will you play as a slim person? It can be difficult if all your friends are overweight and you are the one who has successfully lost weight. They will be envious but may mask it by trying to tempt you to eat cakes and biscuits, drink wine and things to make you put on the weight again.

Fat people and thin people even move differently. Notice what's been changing as you lose weight. How will you sustain it? Missing meals or eating weird foods to lose weight for a wedding or holiday is not sustainable. Switch to a regime that allows for three meals a day that can be eaten in your usual everyday environment. If you're exercising like mad to tone up, think about cutting back to exercise that can be done on a long-term basis. Think ahead and visualize yourself as the size you want to be, and act as if you are that size now so that the transition is seamless.

Putting it all together

When we have achieved our goal, we will have a new identity and this needs to be underpinned in all the levels of change: environment, behaviour, skills, values and beliefs. You will already be starting to do this but you will be more aligned and congruent if you start visualizing your goal and how these levels will support and sustain you in the future. Use a circle of excellence to keep you focused and on track.

11 Delete your criticism

'Every word, facial expression, gesture, or action on the part of a parent gives the child some message about self-worth. It is sad that so many parents don't realize what messages they are sending.' Virginia Satir

'The meeting of two personalities is like the contact of two chemical substances: if there is any reaction, both are transformed.' Carl Jung

'Deletions are the blind spots in our experience.' Joseph O'Connor

'The language you use reflects your internal representation – what's in your mind – and if that language is confused and unspecific, that means your thoughts are too.' Steve Bavister and Amanda Vickers

'The word "deletion" implies that we are chopping out great chunks of reality and throwing them over the side. It is more useful to recognize that our attention is, necessarily, selective and that whatever we are paying attention to will leave a whole lot of other stuff unattended to, and thereby missing, or deleted, from our awareness at that point.' Steve Andreas

Feedback is the response you get from another person to your communication and the response you give as a result of their communication. Both the initial communication and the feedback can be either verbal or non-verbal. In fact, it is said that the non-verbal communication has far more impact than the tone of voice and the tone of the voice has more impact than the words, so, all in all, the words we use come rather late to change whatever impact you have already made non-verbally. We have to take responsibility for our communication ourselves. It is not up to the other person to try to work out what we meant, so it is very important to use feedback as your way of checking that the communication was received as intended. A classic example of **deleting feedback** is when we shrug or dismiss a compliment.

We delete because otherwise we would be overwhelmed by data. It is essential in today's multi-sensory world, with its hundreds of emails and texts, to select what we can cope with at any one time. How we make the selection will depend on our beliefs and values about priorities. When we delete feedback by either ignoring or only noticing part of the verbal or non-verbal reaction to our communication, we miss out on elements of the learning it could offer.

The most extreme form of deleting feedback is to ignore it, of course. Instead of noticing the reaction of the other person, we carry on without noticing it. Imagine communicating with someone who is having a negative reaction to something you are saying but, instead of noticing and changing the subject or the non-verbal behaviour, you carry on. They have given you feedback but you have not realized it. Similarly, if we don't give feedback ourselves when we have some to give, we are denying the other person the opportunity to learn and also the chance to connect and build rapport. Equally, you need to give yourself feedback that you can learn from.

Another deletion is to notice the feedback but only in a vague way, so there are no specifics. Maybe you know that what you're doing is not appreciated or what you're saying isn't going down very well but, instead of checking this out or noticing what precisely the feedback is, you just accept this vague response. When you give feedback, be specific and say what you like and what you'd like to see, hear and experience even more of.

A similar unspecific deletion is when we just notice a comparative, such as a comment going down better than the previous one, but miss out on the way in which it was better so that we are unable to make the next one better, too, and in a specific way. When you give feedback, instead of saying simply 'That was better,' make it clear in what way it was better.

Sometimes, when we get feedback, we notice only whether it is right or wrong; we make a judgement but it lacks detail and the sort of learning that will make a difference next time. Instead of deciding that someone's feedback or response is wrong and therefore of no value, be curious about where they're coming from and what underpins their response.

Another form of deletion is nominalization, which is when we use words like 'organization' or 'society' or 'people', again using vague terms to represent specific people and their specific views. Be clear who you are referring to when you give feedback and, if you are on the receiving end, ask. One example of nominalization is: 'Customers don't like that product.'

Feedback is a gift we can learn so much from. How others respond to us enables us to learn how to communicate more precisely, not offend or upset, but instead delight and create rapport. By being vague about how we give and receive feedback, we deny others the gift and deny ourselves the learning opportunity.

DELETING FEEDBACK AT WORK

As adults we probably receive most of our feedback in a work context via the annual review. Here your boss and possibly colleagues will sit down with you and give you the equivalent of a school report covering every aspect of your job. They will rate you according to how well you have done compared to what is expected of you, based on forecasts perhaps and how this year's performance compares with last year's. Ideally, there will be detail there from which to learn. Look for the specifics throughout the report and ask questions to find out exactly how you did this or that.

Surprisingly, we tend as a culture in the West to shrug off positive feedback, delete it, and concentrate on the criticism. Indeed, the word 'criticism' is even taken to mean something negative, although 'critique' usually means feedback on either positive or negative points. But if you delete your positive feedback, you delete also the possibility of being able to take it on board, develop those positive skills and grow them still further, possibly making a name for yourself in your organization as the 'go to' person for that skill.

There will be opportunities for feedback less formally throughout the year at work, so take them. Give them, too. Ask your colleagues for feedback and ask your customers and clients and be prepared for them to ask for feedback from you as well.

PUTTING DELETION TO GOOD USE

There are times when we need to delete, where we need to select what we pay attention to because otherwise we would get distracted and overwhelmed. We need to speed-read documents to glean the key points.

Sportsmen and women need to focus on their performance and delete distractions – heckling from the crowd, cheers for their opponent and the announcements from another court or the public address system. They know what they need to pay attention to and are trained to focus only on that.

When taking important exams, children and teenagers need to delete noises from other students and focus on their own work. Similarly, when you're working hard in an open-plan office, unless you can delete other people's conversations, it will be difficult to concentrate. Indeed, many who find this hard will bring in their own music and headphones so they can separate themselves from the extraneous noise.

When we are ill or disabled and there are things we can't do, in order to remain upbeat we may delete the pain or discomfort and those things we can't do in order to focus on those things we can do.

Choosing what to delete is usually done unconsciously – we make hundreds, if not thousands, of decisions a day as we focus on what needs to be done. It would be exhausting to bring these choices to our conscious level, however. When communicating with people with whom we want to build rapport – our colleagues, friends, family and loved ones – and when we are doing something that we care about, such as a sport or activity, becoming aware of what we may be deleting and filling in the gaps will give us a richer, fuller learning experience from which to develop.

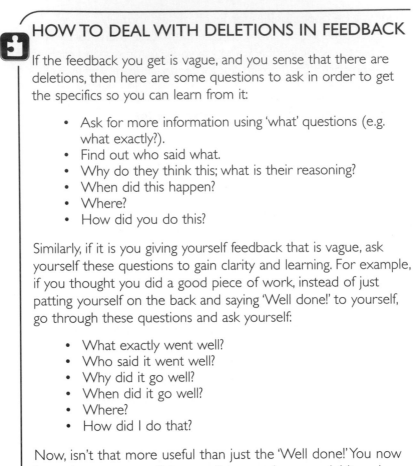

HOW TO DEAL WITH DELETIONS IN FEEDBACK

If the feedback you get is vague, and you sense that there are deletions, then here are some questions to ask in order to get the specifics so you can learn from it:

- Ask for more information using 'what' questions (e.g. what exactly?).
- Find out who said what.
- Why do they think this; what is their reasoning?
- When did this happen?
- Where?
- How did you do this?

Similarly, if it is you giving yourself feedback that is vague, ask yourself these questions to gain clarity and learning. For example, if you thought you did a good piece of work, instead of just patting yourself on the back and saying 'Well done!' to yourself, go through these questions and ask yourself:

- What exactly went well?
- Who said it went well?
- Why did it go well?
- When did it go well?
- Where?
- How did I do that?

Now, isn't that more useful than just the 'Well done!' You now have the structure of the excellence and can model it again and again.

Putting it all together

How and what we delete depends on our values and beliefs, so if you have low self-esteem you will delete anything that contradicts this belief – so you will delete compliments.

If you have a limiting belief about your game of tennis or golf, you will delete examples of great shots and notice only those that support your belief about how bad you are. Be aware of what you delete and, whether you are giving feedback or receiving it, fill in the gaps where the content is vague with questions to gain the specific feedback that will help you – and them – grow.

12 Believe that there's no such thing as failure

> 'I have not failed. I've just found 10,000 ways that won't work.'
> Thomas Edison

> 'Success is not final, failure is not fatal: it is the courage to continue that counts.' Winston Churchill

> 'If doubt or fear that they might lose enters someone's mind and if the other person does not have any fear of losing... then that person will win.' John Newcombe (winner of many Grand Slam tennis tournaments)

> 'There's only one thing that makes dreams impossible to achieve: the fear of failure.' Paulo Coelho

> 'This presupposition is one of the most liberating because once you embrace it you can try all of the things you were once afraid of doing. The more failures you have, the more you learn. So one strategy for learning might be to "fail" more often!' Steve Bavister and Amanda Vickers

For many of us, this last claim seems extraordinary. After all, we have experienced those feelings of rejection (especially as a writer!) – failing exams, failing to get a date, a job, a house or have a baby. Those all certainly feel like failure when you're in the driving seat. Yet, when Bandler and Grinder modelled successful people as they developed NLP back in the 1960s, they discovered that one thing they all had in common was that they viewed failure as feedback and would not countenance it as a full stop but rather as a comma. Imagine if we could take on that belief – how would that change what we do and what we are capable of?

This is one of the presuppositions or beliefs on which NLP is founded and we are encouraged to take this as a given and act 'as if' it is true in everything we set out to do. The reason why it is so important is because, when we believe it to be true, we keep going until we succeed. So how do we do this? What do we do with those feelings that we used to ascribe to failure? We need to reframe them. Reframing is when we take a look at an experience in another way. We get another angle on it.

The angle in the case of failure is that we consider the previous 'failure' feelings as learning instead. In many ways, this is more natural. After all, imagine that you are trying to open a door and initially try the wrong key – you wouldn't give up and go away; you'd try another key and, if none of them worked, you'd go round the back and try the back door. You'd check you had the right house and maybe call the owners as well. If all else failed, depending on the situation, you might even try the windows, too. In short, you'd keep trying and each attempt would tell you something more to help you eventually succeed. Even babies, as they try to walk, don't give up when they fall over; they keep trying and they hold on to furniture and eventually they succeed… otherwise we'd still all be crawling about as adults. Learning, then, is inherent and instinctive, so why do we often give up and decide we've failed?

One of the answers is that we filter our experiences according to our memories, experiences, beliefs and values, then we subconsciously delete, distort and generalize them. We delete by noticing only part of the experience such as just hearing the criticism rather than the praise (do you sometimes shrug off compliments and yet get hurt by the lack of them?). We distort by blowing things out of proportion or imagining that people 'have it in for us'? Generalizations are when we take one experience and kid ourselves that this happens 'all the time' or 'never'. One of the ways we stop ourselves learning from so-called failure is by deleting, distorting and generalizing.

DON'T ACCEPT DEFEAT

When we give up on things very quickly and call it failure, it is often because of a belief we have that we should find things easy and succeed first time. This could be because in the past we have done so. Maybe as a child we used to find things easy, but then as work at school became harder and we couldn't do it so easily we decided we were not so bright after all and gave up instead of finding other ways to understand the subject.

Apart from past experience informing how we frame failure, we can also blame our upbringing. Parents and significant adults in early life can make it difficult for us to pick ourselves up and get going again after disappointments. They can suggest that it's inherited – 'I wasn't any good at maths either' or 'No one in our family ever went to university and it didn't do them any harm.' They might tell you that it isn't important – 'What do you want to speak French for?' or 'Exams aren't everything, you know.' In trying to make you feel better, they may even persuade you that you didn't want to succeed anyway and that it's even an advantage to have failed – 'You're better off staying where you are' or "You wouldn't want the stress of that job.'

In those ways, we get into the habit of accepting defeat and we bow to the pressure of other people wanting to make our life easier or for us to feel good about ourselves instead of persevering until we succeed. It is well known that even a successful novelist like J.K. Rowling was rejected many times before being published – and what a loss it would have been not to have experienced Harry Potter. Sportsmen train daily to achieve success and study their form in minute detail to see where they went wrong and discuss with their trainer how to do it differently next time. This is what we need to do, too.

BE CURIOUS ABOUT THE LEARNING

Where you choose to place your focus will also have an influence on the outcome. When we feel deflated and focus on what has not worked out, we can sometimes fail to notice and learn from what has been successful. We get the balance all wrong. Instead, next time you think something has failed, stop and track through the process, picking out the things that went well so you hold on to them for next time. Take time to learn from what went well. What skills did you apply? Could you have done anything differently to get a better result?

Write down what you've learned from the successes and what you plan to do next time, and only when you feel good about what went well should you look at areas which need a different approach.

Think about those things that went less well – what have you learned? Could you have used these skills you've just identified in those areas to get a different result? How? Run through the structure of what happened, the process rather than the content. How could you change the process next time?

Be curious about the learning.

AHEAD OF THE GAME

In his book *Ahead of the Game*, Jeremy Lazarus explains that sport in many ways is a metaphor for life, so by managing sports defeats or poor performance we can apply this learning more generally. He advocates a four-step approach.

1. **Acknowledge and learn:** Disassociate by mentally stepping away from the event and view it as an impartial observer. What would be the learning here?
2. **Just let go:** Take yourself forward in time and notice how unimportant the mistake was in the context of your life overall. Go back in time and think of other mistakes you've made that you'd forgotten about and take the mental image of the mistake and imagine throwing it into the wind.
3. **Get back into the right state:** Use anchoring to get back into the state you need for the next shot.
4. **Focus on what you want:** When you focus on what you want – good shots, good performance – that's what you get more of.

Putting it all together

There is no such thing as failure. Believe this and you give
yourself all the tools you need to succeed, because you will
be curious about learning from the things that did not go so
well. You will notice what did go well and notice the skills you
have so that they are available to you to apply to those areas
that need work. Open up your awareness of your visual skills
to observe, your auditory skills for listening to feedback, and
your kinaesthetic skills for sensing and acting on them. The
person with the most flexibility controls the system and the
ability to reject failure and embrace learning gives you more
choices. Bandler and Grinder claim that a person with only
one choice is a robot so, unless you want to be a robot, give
yourself more choices and choose to learn from mistakes,
not be brought down by them.

13 Don't distort your feedback

> 'The most dangerous of all falsehoods is a slightly distorted truth.' Georg Lichtenberg

> 'In the world of objects , it makes sense to say that a force acting on an object "makes" it move. However, people are more complex and to claim a cause–effect relationship between one action and another deletes individual choice and all the richness of the relationship.' Joseph O'Connor

> 'People delete, distort and generalize incoming information based on their mental filters, which act largely subconsciously. These filters are beliefs, values, memories, thinking patterns and the state we are in.' Bekki Hill

> 'Distortion is a personal prejudice that twists our perceptions.' Genie Z. Laborde

> 'By learning to challenge our language, we create greater coherence in who we are and we increase the influence we have in all aspects of life.' Sue Knight

We all interpret our world in a unique way based on our own life experiences, values and beliefs. Faced with an overwhelming amount of information, we have to select what we need or want at any one time. When we give or receive feedback it is important not to delete content, distort it or generalize because those three things restrict us from getting the benefit in terms of the learning. Feedback is the response we give and get from communication, either verbal or non-verbal. Distortion is the effect of mind-reading and making assumptions about a person's behaviour rather than checking it out with them.

When we give feedback, it needs to be clear and specific and it needs to be what we think – based on what we have observed rather than on assumptions we make rooted in our view of the world. Distortion occurs when we make 1 + 1 = 3, where the evidence doesn't point to the conclusion we've drawn because we've added something of our own into the mix. An example of this might be 'My children are fighting to annoy me' or 'My boss has given me extra work because he doesn't like me.' You can also recognize this type of distortion where you have sentences joined by the word 'so' or 'therefore' – for example 'He hasn't told me he loves me recently so he must be having an affair' or 'She is playing on her computer, therefore she isn't doing her homework.'

When we add our own meaning, we are distorting the original meaning. It assumes we know better what the intention of the behaviour or communication was. We compare what they say and do with our own map of the world and it becomes our truth. Feedback needs to be given in the spirit of curiosity and respect for the other person's map of the world. What else could they mean? Where someone has presented two linked statements for them, there is an association or meaning in their map of the world. We need to challenge this using clean questions such as 'In what way…' or 'And how is… and that's like what?' – we're looking to understand how 1 + 1 = 3 in their map.

When we are given feedback, the same thing applies. Be curious about the content, what they have observed and question any assumptions they have made that have distorted it. This is all part of the feedback because you need to know what it was that you communicated that gave them this impression – you, after all, are responsible for your communication.

Reverse mind-reading is also distortion. This is when someone says, 'If you knew me…' or 'If you cared about me, you would…' or 'You should know that…' Here you are criticizing someone for not responding in the way they should, yet you have never told them what you wanted.

Another type of distortion is cause and effect, where we offer feedback to someone that they 'make' us feel a certain way. This isn't true because someone can't *make* you feel something; this is your choice. However, what interests us is how this can be so for the other person, so we'd ask 'How exactly did I do that?' or 'How did X do that exactly?'

Presuppositions are another way we can distort feedback. Here, we make assumptions about how 'people' should behave or what is expected of us, again based on our own map of the world. Expressions like 'How pleased will you be when we get this contract?' assumes you will be pleased, which of course you may be, but it is still nevertheless a presupposition. Lots of 'How… is that / How will you feel when…' phrases make assumptions and this is often done in celebrity interviews to lead the way the interviewee will respond, but has no place in feedback where an open exchange is preferable. One phrase that you'll often hear at work is, 'When shall we have our next meeting on this?', which presupposes that there needs to be one and thus more time is taken up having meetings without questioning the need to have one.

PARENTS AND CHILDREN

Parents frequently distort feedback to and from their children, partly because the relationship is so intense and emotional that it becomes difficult to objectively observe behaviour. There is a huge amount of mind-reading that goes on because parents 'unecologically' assume that they can do this because the child is theirs, of their own flesh and blood, and that therefore they ought to be able to read their mind. Of course they can't.

When children disobey their parents, it isn't usually because they want to 'make' them angry or upset, even though this is often what parents say. Parents often take the action of their children at a very personal level, assuming they are involved when usually they are not. Next time you respond to your child, feed back what you have noticed without putting any interpretation on it from your own very different map of the world. Be curious about their map as you tell them how you feel about what they have done or said. By taking this slightly more disassociated stance, you allow for improved rapport and connection. You also model for them how to give feedback and how to receive it.

When your children are giving you feedback that seems distorted, question the assumptions using clean questions such as 'And how exactly did I do that? or 'And how exactly did I make you feel this?'

PRECISION QUESTIONS

Grinder and Bandler developed what they called 'precision questions' in order to challenge and influence the constraints that people put on themselves. They challenge the perceptions we form about ourselves and the way we express these patterns of deletions, distortions and generalizations in our language, both internally and externally, when we talk to others.

- Who said this?/According to whom?/Which people?
- In what way?
- How/why did they do that?
- Better/more than what?
- Compared to what?
- How do you know?
- How does… mean… ?
- What is your evidence for that?

A DEADLY COCKTAIL

In romantic relationships, there's a tendency to 'overthink' what our partners say. In our anxiety to please and to be loved, we are vulnerable and easily distort what is said and done, overlaying it with our map of the world. And because men and women (and indeed men and men and women and women) are notoriously different from each other, this can lead to some classic misunderstandings. Add a few children into the equation and hormones, and soon one has a deadly cocktail of presuppositions and cause-and-effect situations.

Are any of these familiar?

- 'He's bought me flowers again this month; he must be feeling guilty about something'
- 'He bought me the wrong size; he thinks I'm fat.'

- 'She didn't reply to my text; she doesn't care.'
- 'She forgot my birthday, deliberately.'
- 'You make me so angry.'
- 'You don't love me anymore'.
- 'When are you going to stop spending so much on clothes?'
- 'When are you going to do more to help around the house?'

What we're doing is putting our own interpretation on to their behaviour. If we had done that thing, then that is what it would mean according to our map of the world. What we need to find out is what it means in their map of the world. In the last two examples of 'when' questions, we are making our own assumption that they spend too much or don't help enough. That may not be their view at all. It's difficult to move on from two different maps like this because it's like two different languages that don't make sense to each other. However, when an observation is made instead, then one has the opportunity to tell the other person what is meant so one can understand and talk about the behaviour itself rather than the interpretation of it.

Putting it all together

We cannot possibly take in all the data that surrounds us, and when we give feedback we inevitably reflect our own distortion of the event based on our map of the world. How we interpret what has been said or done makes sense to us given our values and beliefs; indeed, had we done or said this thing, that is what we would have meant by it. But we each have a different map so, whether you are giving or receiving feedback, be aware that you are making assumptions and interpreting, making judgements and assuming cause and effect… distorting. Use precision questions to explore the other person's map, and experience a deeper level of communication and greater rapport.

14 Beware of generalizing your feedback

'Generalizations are linguistic fluff that clogs the works of clear communication.' Joseph O'Connor and John Seymour

 'It is by developing ourselves that we influence others.' Sue Knight

'The generalizations of all, every, and always can block off avenues of escape from problems, avenues that offer unexamined or unnoticed solutions.' Genie Z. Laborde

'Fritz Perls, the originator of Gestalt therapy, used to respond to clients who said, "I can't..." by saying, "Don't say I can't, say I won't!" This rather ferocious reframe immediately shifts the client's stuck state to a state of being able to at least acknowledge the possibility of choice.' Joseph O'Connor and John Seymour

'People tell me with absolute certainty they don't trust themselves. Or they tell me that they decided absolutely that they can't make good decision. You know what, it's impossible for anyone to tell you anything that's a generalization about themselves that won't destroy itself including that one...'
Richard Bandler

Generalization is when one takes one idea and attributes it in a general way to apply to all of the category. So 'You're late' becomes 'You're always late' or 'Why can you never get anywhere on time?' These statements are rarely true and it is in challenging them that you get the more precise learning.

Feedback is a gift and can bring profound learning for the giver and receiver when it is specific and given with curiosity for the other person's map of the world.

The first type of generalization is what we call **'universal truths'**. These involve words like 'always', 'never', 'everyone', 'no one'. When you hear words like this, your response needs to be a questioning look and repeating the word in that tone in order to elicit some clarification:

'You're always nagging me to do the washing-up.'

'Always?'

or

'You never remember my birthday.'

'Never?'

As a result, you will find out what lies behind the generalization and also when the exceptions occur. The learning will be in these exceptions. When, for example, do they not nag and when do they remember? Find these out and there will be the learning from the feedback. Delegate, dump or do.

Generalizations often stem from childhood when children were told things in the simplest way for economy of explanation and to get the point across quickly and without discussion – for example 'Never talk to strangers', 'Always look before crossing the road', 'No one picks their nose at the table.' We grow out of needing these simple rules, and indeed networking events would be rather quiet if no one ever spoke to a stranger. These generalizations can often become habits founded on beliefs about how to be a good employee such as 'Never be late for work' or beliefs about health and hygiene such as 'Always brush your teeth' or 'Always wash your hands after using the toilet.' These types of generalization short-cut a lot of thinking because they become automatic habits. After all, if every day we have to consider whether or not to brush our teeth, we probably would be late for work. Sometimes generalizations can become prejudices, though, such as 'All bankers are crooked' or 'All black people are good runners.'

Racism is another form of generalization – people judge a whole race as being one thing or another. These sorts of short cut cause wars.

Another generalization is what we call **'drivers'** or **'statements of need'**, where we deny ourselves choice – for example, when we say we 'have to' do something. For example, 'I have to finish writing this chapter' or 'You must correct that appalling grammar' or 'You should go and see the doctor.' Challenge these types of generalization by asking 'why' or 'according to whom?' and liberate yourself by adding some choice – 'What do you want to do?'

The third type of generalization is called a **'limiter'** or **'stopper'**, which again restricts your choice – this time by introducing a limiting belief, 'I can't'. These expressions imply that it is not possible to do it, yet in truth you actually mean that you don't yet know how to do it and could learn. When we give feedback by saying, 'I can't understand why you did this or that' or 'I can't write this report,' or when someone says this to us, we need to challenge it and question what's stopping us and open up the possibilities by asking 'what would happen if I did?'.

DELEGATE, DUMP OR DO

When you find yourself saying 'I must do…' or 'I have to…', then stop and decide whether you want to or not. Do the things that bring you pleasure, the things you believe are important and add value to your life, and do the things that draw you closer to your goal. You know the things you want to do.

Now you're left with the rest. Some could be done by someone else. There are people around you who have an investment in this thing that you feel should be done, so spread the load and get someone else to do it by asking them. Many people find it hard to delegate because they want to control how a task is done and don't really trust that anyone else can do it as well as they can. If that's you, decide whether you can delegate both what is done and how it is done. Maybe you will even find a better way of doing it in the future?

The rest you can dump because it has no value to you. We are not judged by how busy we are, how fast we run about the office, how many emails we get every day, how often our mobile beeps to say we have a message or how many followers we have on Twitter. You judge yourself against what is important to you, who and what you want to be.

'I CAN'T'

Children frequently tell you they 'can't' do something. They might do this to save time; after all, you can do it much more quickly (they are delegating) or you can help them, which gives them precious attention as well as having to make less effort themselves. However, 'can't' is a generalization and an example of a limiting belief or stopper. By helping them or by doing it for them, you are confirming their limiting belief that indeed they really can't do it. They are generalizing when they say this because, although they may feel they can't do it at this moment, it doesn't mean they won't be able to do it once you've shown them how or if they keep trying.

Ask them what they need in order to be able to do it. Do they need time, more information, a demonstration, reassurance that they will be able to do it if they keep trying? Perhaps they've done something similar before and need to be reminded that they could do that thing that is like what they're trying now. For example, if they are struggling with some difficult homework, say 'Do you remember when you were struggling last week with something, you went on to something else and then came back to it afresh and could see how to do it then?' – or whatever their strategy had been.

When someone says they can't do something, it does not mean that it is impossible to do it. There are some things that are impossible, of course: 'If pigs could fly' is what we say sometimes to express that something is impossible. In most cases, though, the word 'can't' is a limiting belief and can be challenged by asking 'What if you could?', to encourage the person to consider the possibility of being able to do it. We could also ask, 'What's stopping you from doing it?' to find out what the barrier is.

FIND THE EXCEPTION

We need to generalize in many areas because, if we treated every event as a unique one, we'd take ages to do anything – for example, if we didn't generalize that cars start with the turn of a key we'd get into a car and wonder how to get it to start. This probably seems absurd and it is, of course, but how much can we generalize without it becoming problematic to good rapport?

At a subconscious level, we therefore sort for difference and we do this at a phenomenal speed, so as we go to the car, one we are not familiar with, our brain asks how likely is it that this car will start in a different way from all the cars we have driven before. Given that there are no obvious signs that it is different, we assume sameness and generalize. If, however, we were given a card instead of a key then alarm bells would ring that this was different and we would perhaps ask how to start it.

In communication, and therefore in feedback, our alarm bells ring when we hear something that sounds unlikely, such as 'I never do anything right.' Find out whether they have ever done anything right: find the exception and question the generalization. It is when you find the pattern for the exception that they will have the structure of their excellence – so what did they do on that occasion, and how did they get it right then? Do that again.

Putting it all together

Generalizations limit our choices and possibilities by assuming that, if something has happened once, it will always be so; or, if one person is like this, so will everyone else be. These generalizations are not facts but are perceptions from one map of the world – just as saying we can't do something or must do something limits our choices. When you hear a generalization, challenge it to help the other person (perhaps you have a menacing inner voice that generalizes), and find the structure of their excellence and the possibilities that they are closing down.

15 Change your beliefs through feedback

'To improve is to change; to be perfect is to change often.'
Winston Churchill

'Any single person's viewpoint will have blind spots caused by their habitual ways of perceiving the world, their perceptual filters... How can we shift our perceptions to get outside our own limited world view?' **John Seymour**

'In order to make your communication more effective, you measure it on the response that you get. You've got to take responsibility for your communication and, if you're not getting the result you want, you need to change what you're doing.'
Tony Robbins

'All that we are arises with our thoughts. With our thoughts we make the world.' **Buddha**

'If you say to yourself "It's difficult to get up in the morning", "It's hard to cease smoking", then you are already using hypnotic suggestions on yourself...' **Richard Bandler**

Sometimes we hold on to old, outdated beliefs about ourselves because they have become our identity and what we are known for in the family or at work – for example, 'That's Frank – he doesn't like change, does he?' or 'Typical, mate; we know you like a good argument.' Perhaps we even reinforce them ourselves by saying 'Oh, you know me and deadlines' or 'You know detail isn't my thing.' Instead of continuing to accept these limiting beliefs about yourself, how about instead becoming aware of feedback and giving yourself the opportunity to change these beliefs?

In the introduction you were given the presuppositions that the original NLP Masters found to be true for their models of excellence. Here they are again. Read through the list and select one belief that you'd like to have right now in a particular area of your life.

- Everyone makes the best choice available to them – accept, understand and forgive.
- There is no failure, only feedback – accept mistakes as a learning opportunity.
- Behind every behaviour is a positive intention – be curious, find it and learn from it.
- The map is not the territory – what you feel is only one way of looking at things; there are other ways that might prove more useful.
- The meaning of the communication is its effect – take responsibility for what and how you communicate.
- We already have all the resources we need – tap into all your resources and divert them to where they are needed.
- The person with the most flexibility has the most influence – the more choices of how to respond we have, the better.
- Mind and body are one – what affects one affects the other.
- If one person can do a thing, anyone can – this is what modelling is for.
- There is a solution to every problem – be curious to find it.
- What is true of someone else is true for us, too – what we notice in others we have too; that's how we recognize it.
- If you always do what you've always done, you will always get what you've always got – it's you who have to change if you want a different result.

Now focus just on that one belief and ask yourself whether this has even been a belief you have held or whether perhaps it was true for you once but no longer. Think about whether it is a belief you hold in one aspect of your life. When has someone given you the feedback that showed evidence of you holding this belief? Perhaps you can imagine having a belief that is similar to this or you know someone who has this belief. Can you imagine what it would be like to hold this belief? What would have to be true for you to hold this belief? Really focus on the belief and make it real for you by picturing yourself in a situation where you might hold this belief. If you are visual, creating an image will work well for making it come to life for you; if you are auditory, then you'll want to imagine someone commenting on you when you hold this belief; and if you are kinaesthetic, then you'll want to imagine how people will react to you – what they'll do.

As you make this belief real, imagine acting as if it is real now. It's like trying on a coat and walking around in it. How does it feel? How do people react to you? Notice what feedback you get and ask for feedback.

INTEGRATING BELIEFS

If there is a belief you want someone else to have, perhaps a child or a colleague, you can give them feedback when you feel they are exhibiting this belief in order to emphasize it for them and signpost it in case they haven't noticed. For example, if you want your child to take responsibility rather than relying on you, decide what belief you'd like them to have in this area. Suppose we describe the desired belief as 'It is my responsibility for having all the right things for school in the morning.' Wording the belief in your own mind is quite important so you know what you are looking for evidence of.

Now observe. Be ready to point out evidence of the belief and use the exact words. So when you see him gathering his things together you say: 'I'm glad to see you are taking responsibility for having all the right things for school in the morning.' If anything is forgotten, you can still use this belief: 'It's great to see that you are taking responsibility for having all the right things for school in the morning and I'm wondering if you need a…'

You can integrate this belief at the identity level by saying, 'I'm proud that you are someone who takes responsibility for having all the right things for school in the morning.' When children integrate a belief into their identity, it then becomes 'what they do' because that is 'who they are', rather than simply doing it because you've told them to.

DITCH OUTDATED BELIEFS

Sometimes people are reluctant to change a belief because they feel they have had it for so long that it is like an old friend or a comfortable pair of slippers. Yet they know that without this belief they could get that new job, take that risk, ask that girl out. When having the belief might hold you back from a new opportunity, it may be time to look for ways to ditch it and replace it with something more useful.

Decide what belief you want to have and be curious about where you have it currently. If you want to be organized in one part of your life, look for organization in another part – because that's where you'll find the skills you need. Maybe the belief you want is something you used to have, in which case, again, start looking at the time when you had the belief and piece together the strategy you used then.

Feedback is evidence, examples, experience of something. When we look hard for evidence of a belief, we can usually find it because we already have all the resources we need. If you are finding it hard to find evidence of the belief you require, ask friends and family 'When have you seen me have the belief that…?'

BECOME YOUR OWN FEEDBACK

When you play a sport, much of your feedback will be non-verbal – for example the sound of the ball on the racket or the ground, the sound of your boot kicking the ball, or the bat hitting the ball. You know what a good shot sounds, looks and feels like. So much feedback is non-verbal, yet we tend to focus on verbal feedback, listening out for specific words and phrases that will be evidence of what we are trying to achieve. But when someone says 'Good shot!' and you know it wasn't because you have listened to the sound it made and can see it was not as good as you hoped, then we are quick to dismiss the feedback because it doesn't concur with our own view.

Start to become your own feedback by setting desirable outcomes for each shot and giving yourself feedback on each one, the good and the less good. Remember to start with a positive comment – 'I hit the ball in the right place' – then what could be better – 'I need to hit it harder next time' – and finish with a good point – 'I'm making progress.' The last part of the feedback is the belief part, so make sure when you complete your feedback loop you focus on the belief that you are working on regarding your performance.

Putting it all together

Ignore people who say that it is difficult to change your beliefs – because it isn't. We change beliefs all the time as we experience new things, learn more about the world and develop ourselves personally. You can find evidence or feedback on nearly every belief you could have, somewhere in your life, so be open to it and question yourself to increase your flexibility. The more choices you have about the beliefs you want to espouse, the more control you will have over your life.

16

Give feedback that your staff can learn from

'A few well-chosen words at just the right time can transform a person's life.' Joseph O'Connor

'Our primary objective must be to understand what the performer/learner needs in order to perform the task well, and to ask, say, or do whatever it takes to help him meet that need. Our own wish to be in control or to display our superior knowledge, or simply our laziness to give up old habits and change, will need to be set aside if we want him to perform. It is hard to break the prevailing mold of behavior, but break it we must.' John Whitmore

'Praise is another form of feedback. It tends to be sparingly offered and hungrily received in the workplace, where criticism abounds.' John Whitmore

'When managers give feedback on key, specific behaviors and make sure these behaviors get corrected, employees will focus, improve performance, and build positive momentum for further improvement.' Alan Ovson

'It is by learning to love and thrive on feedback that we can excel in the spontaneity of today's business climate. And by thriving on it we are in the best position to respond with flexibility to whatever arises.' Sue Knight

Feedback is the response you get from what you do or say, and that can be verbal or non-verbal and it can range from a smile or a laugh through to a detailed report. As an employer or manager, you are responsible for how you choose to give your staff feedback and how you do it will either motivate them to perform better or it will upset them to the extent that they won't want to work for you any more. Expertly done, feedback will ensure your staff's loyalty and support as well as improving their performance.

A fundamental principle to bear in mind when giving feedback to staff is that there is no failure, only feedback. What you are offering them is the chance to learn how you perceived their performance or their work. It is not a fact, but it is how it seemed to you; others may indeed have perceived it differently. The map is not the territory. So your state of mind has to be one of curiosity and objectivity when approaching feedback. What could they have meant when they did this or that? What was their desirable outcome? If you're not getting the results you want from your staff, you should first examine your own communication style. How are you communicating? Could you change it and get a different result? Are you giving enough detail or too much detail? Are you giving too much choice or not enough choice? Are you telling them what you do want rather than what you don't want? Are you showing your appreciation and giving positive feedback when they do well so they know what you expect? Often, when we speak to someone we think only about what we want to say, the content, when it's the process that needs work.

Today we have very efficient means of communicating, via text and email, both of which are immediate, but feedback should be delivered *personally*. Find a time soon after the event to have a one-to-one with the staff member and give them the chance to respond, if not immediately, then at another time after they've thought about what you have said.

We tend to notice character traits we have ourselves, so when we point out something to a member of staff we need also to consider how it could be true for us as well. When we do that, we could take this one step further and be curious about why and how we too do this thing, because this will help us understand why they do and enable us to give more insightful and actionable feedback. Again, though, we need to own the feedback and say 'When I do this it's because… what about you, how is it for you?'

PRAISE

Praise is an essential form of feedback. How often do you take the time to tell your staff that they've done well?

It's not enough just to say, 'Well done.' This is too vague. How do they know which aspect of the work they did was 'well done'; maybe it was about the speed or the accuracy, the presentation... who knows? They certainly don't, so point it out.

When someone has done some good work, find one or two positive aspects of it to comment on and personalize it. Own the praise by mentioning the great things that you noticed about their work (not about them personally) or something they did. Add the element of appreciation so that it comes across as sincere.

Praise is particularly welcome when you mention specifically something you know they either find difficult or something you know they have been working on. This helps them to know when they are getting it right and when they have made an improvement. It's an essential part of their learning.

When we focus on the good results, we tend to get more of them as that's where we're putting our attention.

On the subject of praise, how do *you* take praise? Because this will affect how your staff receive it from you. If you just shrug it off as we are wont to do, then they will, too, and it won't have worked as feedback. Set a good example by accepting praise from others as you'd like others to receive it from you.

GETTING INTO RAPPORT

Feedback is best received when you are in rapport with the person to whom you are giving feedback. To do this, make sure that you first arrange a time that suits them to give your feedback and that you don't do it at the end of the day when they're rushing to catch a train.

We get into rapport by matching their body language – how they're standing or sitting, how they hold their head, what they're doing with their legs and arms. You have to be careful not to do this slavishly, otherwise it looks as if you're making fun of them; if you do it naturally, however, they will feel at ease and unthreatened.

Think about how what you have to say to them is also true for you in some way – this gives you a connectedness in your thinking.

Eye contact is really important for maintaining rapport, as it shows that you genuinely care about giving them the learning.

FEEDBACK STRUCTURE

Here are some important tips for getting the structure right.

1. Establish that it is appropriate for you to be giving feedback as a manager or employer. However, while you are responsible for your employee's work, you are not their friend or partner, so feedback of a personal nature should be avoided unless it affects their work.
2. Choose a moment when you and they aren't rushed and have time to give to the conversation, so not just as they're leaving to go home or to a meeting. Also, if you're not feeling good about something they have done, you may want to allow time to cool off before giving feedback in order to take the emotion out of the situation.
3. Let the person know that you want to give them some feedback so that they can prepare themselves and focus on what you have to say.
4. Assuming it is within your remit, own the feedback rather than suggesting it comes from other people – unless of course this is relevant, such as feedback from a client or supplier that they need to hear and wouldn't hear direct from them. Use 'I' and talk about what you have observed, focusing on the behaviour rather than the person (e.g. 'I have noticed…') and avoid the temptation to mind-read (e.g. 'You've obviously …')
5. Make sure you have all the facts and allow them to fill in the gaps in your knowledge and respond to the feedback with their own conclusions about remedial action.
6. Keep it formal and objective without getting emotional or personal.

Putting it all together

There are often systems in place within organizations that allow us to collect feedback from our suppliers, clients, colleagues, managers, customers and staff. You could probably make a list of the different types used by your own organization and then note alongside how each one could be improved such that you would get the learning from it that would move the organization forward to a better competitive position. Are there parts of the organization that don't get feedback at all? How could this be done most effectively? A climate of regular expert feedback creates an environment where colleagues feel supported in their personal and career growth.

17 Give hypnotic feedback to change behaviour

'To restrict yourself to the conscious resources of the person who comes to you will guarantee a long, tedious and probably ineffective process. Conscious is defined as whatever you are aware of at a moment in time. Unconscious is everything else.'
Richard Bandler

'Actions speak louder than words. So if a golfer says that he wants to improve his putting, yet does not spend much time practising, the coach could complain, moan, cajole, shout or use whatever approaches a coach may traditionally use. An additional approach would be for the mental skills coach to get curious about the lack of practice and to ask about the positive intention of not practising putting.' Jeremy Lazarus

'Words sculpt our inner world and subsequently shape our outer world. What we say to ourselves (our inner dialogue) has an influence on what we see, hear and feel. Similarly , our spoken words influence not only ourselves but also our listeners. It is vital that we take responsibility for the effect we create with our language if we want to maximise our influence. In other words, the meaning of our communication is indeed its effect.' Sue Knight

'Hypnotic language (sometimes referred to as soft language) is very effective in a coaching context, particularly when you want someone to search inside to find their own solutions, rather than impose or directly suggest ideas.' Richard Churches and Roger Terry

'Words like wonder, curious, know and understand have a particular value because they make it possible to ask questions to which no response is expected. A message can therefore be communicated in an indirect manner.' Steve Bavister and Amanda Vickers

One of the original influencers of NLP was Milton Erickson who contributed hugely to the area of family therapy and language. His own particular area of expertise was hypnosis, which he first used intuitively after contracting polio as a teenager. Unable to speak, he relied on non-verbal communication and learned how he could use muscle memory to instruct his body to mend, so that eventually he did manage to walk with a cane and talk. He went on to study the subconscious and how using hypnotic language could change behaviour.

The Milton Model that we'll be covering here is a language pattern that is described by Bandler and Grinder as being 'artfully vague'. We are not talking here about hypnotizing people to do things they don't want to do as entertainment. The sort of hypnotic state we are talking about here is a state of unawareness, the sort of state we are in when we do something subconsciously like flick a hair away from our eye or drive without noticing where we are because it's a route we take daily.

The reason why hypnotic language is so useful in behaviour change is that when questions are asked that make sense because they are specific and void of deletions, generalizations and distortions, we answer them with our left brain and answer them sensibly, giving rational reasons for our behaviour that we then try to justify and explain. When, instead, we ask the question in a vague way that the other person can barely make sense of, they have to delve into the more creative right brain to fill in the gaps and make some sense of it, but can't because there isn't enough information to know which bit of the answer is needed from all the possible ones in their subconscious. What comes out will therefore probably be more useful material to work with and offer more possibilities for behaviour change.

It was Milton's belief that there was a positive intention behind every behaviour, however bizarre it might appear to someone else.

We have to honour the intention but change the behaviour. To do this, we first find out what the purpose is of the behaviour. We don't use the word 'why' to ask the question because that tends to result in a defensive, rationalized response that won't reflect the underlying positive intention, possibly because the person might not even be aware of it themselves. Better questions are: 'What's the purpose of...?', 'What does... do for you?', 'What does... get for you?', 'For what purpose do you do/want...?'

The next step is to use the answers from step one – in other words, the purpose – and ask how else that purpose could be met with different behaviour: 'How else could you...?' It is important to use their words, not your own, which may be your interpretation of their purpose. Keep encouraging them to come up with other ways to meet their purpose until they have a list.

The final stage is to look at the options together and decide which would be the most appropriate to take. It is an NLP presupposition that people do the best they can, given their own map of the world, so when someone's behaviour does not seem to be a good choice (or even your own), by helping them to understand their map by being curious, we can find alternative behaviours that meet the same intention. Hypnotic language paves the way by being non-judgemental and vague. Here are some other examples of language patterns that have a behaviour-change effect.

EMBEDDED COMMANDS

Parents and teachers may be interested to learn that the word 'don't' is an embedded command. This is because our unconscious mind seeks out the command in the sentence and ignores the rest, so when a teacher tells you 'Don't be worried about this test', you will be worried because in effect that is what you've been told to do. When a parent calls out anxiously as a child walks along a wall, 'Don't look down!' they probably will. We may not have thought about these things until they were suggested, but we have to consider them because otherwise we can't make sense of what has been said. In other words, the child has to consider whether or not they are worried about the test in order to understand what the teacher has said and when they do that they will get worried.

In the gym, trainers shout out 'Don't stop!' and 'Don't give up!' when 'Keep going' would be more effective. When you want someone to do something or when you are managing your own inner dialogue, focus on what you do want.

The 'don't' embedded command is a negative example, and positive ones that work well usually start with 'I'm wondering when you…' or 'I don't know whether you…', both of which sound vague and slightly dreamy or trance-like, which gently draws in the other person to be curious with you and want to consider the possibility.

In a behaviour context, saying to an employee, 'I'm wondering when you will begin to feel motivated,' assumes they will feel motivated and by preceding it with 'I'm wondering' it becomes an embedded command to become motivated. They feel compelled to respond, even though there was no direct question.

You can use embedded commands in direct questions, though, and you do this by assuming the answer you want while apparently asking a question. For example, 'What time will you stop this behaviour?' commands them to stop and assumes they will stop – you have hypnotically suggested it to them, which will be more effective than simply telling them to stop.

When you want to use this type of approach for behaviour change, mark it out by pausing before and after and raising your voice for the actual embedded command.

DOUBLE BINDS

This is another hypnotic pattern and can be used to effect behaviour change by offering someone, or indeed yourself, two options, both of which assume they will do what you want. Salespeople will be familiar with this in the way they close: 'Do you want to place an order today or later this week?' Notice that the embedded command is that they place an order. Similarly, in a school or home context when you want a child to do something, it is often more effective to give them perceived choice – for example, 'I'm wondering whether you'd like to read before or after Sally.' We've embedded the command that they'd like to read. 'George, would you like to do your homework before or after tea?' assumes homework will be done.

Similarly, the word 'and' links two components in a hypnotic way to change behaviour. It works best when one of the components is something they are currently doing and the other is something you'd like them to do. This puts the listener into a 'yes' state from the first part, which they carry forward to the second without thinking. An example would be: 'You are reading this and are wondering how to put it into practice at work tomorrow.' Double binds often include words like 'as' or 'while' – for example, 'As we talk about this report and think about how you will present it to the board…'

Another example uses the gerund as the first part of the sentence: 'Sitting here quietly filling in the answers to our geography questions makes us realize what a lot we know about rivers' will lead students to feel confident that they know a lot about rivers.

MIND-READING

There are many ways in which mind-reading, when used in communication, can lead to loss of rapport, but in the context of hypnotic language it can lead to behaviour change when done with integrity and curiosity.

In this language pattern we make suggestions like this: 'You're probably wondering how to clear up the mess you've made.' They probably weren't but they are now, now that you've planted the idea in their head as a suggestion.

Another variation on this is covering all bases, where we make sure everyone is included in our targeting: 'I know some of you have read this report in its entirety, some have read bits of it and, for others, it is all new.'

Finally, the 'yes' tag, which is probably already familiar, is another mind-reading pattern that prompts a positive response. The pattern is Fact + Fact + Fact + Embedded command + Yes tag. It looks like this: 'It's lunchtime, we have finished the slides for the presentation and we still have the script to write, so now would be a good time to allocate the tasks for the presentation, wouldn't it?' It helps to nod when you add the 'yes tag'.

Putting it all together

Indirect approaches like those taught by Erickson work extremely well for behaviour change because they respect the individual and are non-confrontational. They assume that there is a positive intention and that we are curious and care about it and want to find it in order to explore other options to meet it, which will change the behaviour. Through indirect statements including embedded commands, we gently make suggestions to others for how to change their behaviour and assume that this is what they want to do – which paves the way for them to feel they have their own permission to change it.

18 Use the feedback sandwich

'Failure is just a way of describing a result you did not want. You can use the results you get to redirect your efforts. Feedback keeps the goal in view. Failure is a dead end.'
Joseph O'Connor and John Seymour

'It is by learning to love and thrive on feedback that we can excel in the spontaneity of today's business climate. And by thriving on it we are in the best position to respond with flexibility to whatever arises.' Sue Knight

'Every word, facial expression, gesture, or action on the part of a parent gives the child some message about self-worth. It is sad that so many parents don't realize what messages they are sending.' Virginia Satir

'Feedback is the breakfast of champions.' Ken Blanchard

'When making feedback sandwiches, supervisors can be either chefs or cooks, and assertive, skillful communication differentiates the two. Assertive supervisors (the chefs) express their thoughts and feelings directly, respect the person and address the behavior. Not all supervisors are assertive; some (the cooks) are passive or aggressive'. Anne Dohrenwend, Ph.D.

Think of giving feedback as a gift that you are offering someone. Just like any present, you want the other person to like it, to realize that you've thought about what they'd like and you've taken the trouble to buy it and give it to them. Also, like a gift, you wouldn't throw it at them or leave it somewhere for them to find; you would wait for a good opportunity and then present it to them at a time when they aren't busy doing something else and at a time when you know they will be receptive. The 'feedback sandwich' is the name we give to the structure of feedback that is given and received in the spirit of a gift.

We use a feedback sandwich to allow us to give feedback in a resourceful manner, in rapport, so that both giver and receiver feel good about the experience. We want the recipient of the feedback to know we care and want them to use the feedback in order to achieve a more successful outcome next time. Feedback is a process whereby we learn more about what we've done so we can do more of what works and less of what doesn't. When we think of a stand-up comic, for example, they get instant feedback from their gags. The ones that get a laugh are the ones that stay in their routine and the ones that don't are removed. Similarly, a sportsperson will get immediate feedback from their shot because it will be either in or out, on target or off. A tennis player may know just from the sound of the ball on the racquet whether the shot was good or not and where the ball will land as a result.

In order for the recipient to make good use of the feedback, they need to know that it is a gift of learning and we do this by using a sandwich structure. Like a sandwich, there are three parts to the technique and, like a sandwich, the 'meat' – or work to be done – is in the middle.

Many of us find giving feedback a tricky business. Instead of venturing into what can be a quagmire of potential hurt and offence, we stay silent, hoping that the other person somehow knows instinctively how we feel about what they have done or said. At best, this is optimistic. At worst, we communicate our feedback non-verbally in a way that can be misinterpreted and be just as hurtful without the opportunity to respond and get the learning. In this chapter we learn how to tackle this sticky business, so that, whether you are giving feedback in a formal business environment or an educational one, bringing up children or developing your relationship, by following these guidelines you will learn to tread a more resourceful path.

MAKING YOUR SANDWICH

The essence of the feedback sandwich is that the lesson is the 'filling' in the sandwich and that either side of it is something positive to cushion it.

The **first part** therefore is to say something positive. Be curious about what the other person is doing – the thing about which you want to give feedback – and identify their positive intention. This is what you might comment on to start with. For example, 'I can see you're making a huge effort here…' or 'I really appreciate what you're doing…', 'It's great that …' The purpose of this introduction is to get them 'on side'. They need to know that you mean well and are prepared to see the best in them. You may also refer to something they did recently that was a good example of what you're looking for from them.

The **second part** of your feedback sandwich is the part where you want them to take some learning. Now you tell them what you'd like to see less of or more of, how you think they could improve or do the thing better. It can be very tempting to precede this section with the word 'but'. This is because, having just said something positive, we want to qualify it with our words of advice or feedback, so the word 'but' does tend to trip off the tongue. However, this is best avoided because you may notice that everything before the 'but' becomes unheard when you do this and the thing you say after the 'but' is amplified. This isn't what we want, because we need the other person to pay equal attention to all three parts of the sandwich; we don't want to annihilate them and give them cause to feel terrible. In that state, in any case, they'd be unlikely to accept the feedback; they'd be more likely to feel defensive. Instead, then, replace this word with 'and', leading neatly from the initial positive comment into the part where you want them to take some learning.

The **third part** of the feedback sandwich is to finish with words of encouragement so that the other person knows that what was said was meant well and that it was given in rapport. You might say something like 'Overall, I thought you did a great job' or 'I look forward to working with you next time.' It is important that the interaction finishes on a positive note where the feedback has been delivered and well received.

HOW TO SERVE YOUR FEEDBACK SANDWICH

In her article for *Family Practice Management* (Nov–Dec 2002), published by the American Academy of Family Physicians, Dr Anne Dohrenwend gives her tips on how to serve your feedback sandwich like a chef, assertively:

1. **Be prepared:** Take time to collect your thoughts, avoid generalizations such as 'You always do…' or 'You never…' and identify the problem behaviour. Give feedback when you are feeling calm and focused and clear about the facts.
2. **Be specific:** Identify the 'keep behaviours' that you'd like to see more of and be specific about the behaviours you want them to stop or do less of. Judge the behaviour, not the person.
3. **Suggest corrections:** Rather than leave the recipient empty-handed, offer alternative behaviours to replace the problem behaviour or, if you think it's important for them to come up with a solution, then take the time to brainstorm options.
4. **Own your own opinions:** Use 'I' statements owning your own feedback rather than suggest that this is what 'others' are saying.
5. **Realize your boundaries:** Do you have the right to give feedback on this behaviour? Stay within your own area of responsibility whether that be professional or personal, because when you stray into an area where you don't have the right to give feedback it won't be well taken.
6. **Know yourself:** Avoid transferring your own personal feelings about success or failure and give balanced, accurate feedback.
7. **Be dramatic:** Use good eye contact, shoulder-to-shoulder posture, an open stance and a little drama, because feedback delivered in a monotonous voice will have no impact. If you're making a small point, use a gentle voice and small gestures; and if it's a major point, use pauses, inflection and a louder voice.

8. **Be real:** While a little drama makes the sandwich palatable, baloney will make it disingenuous and it will be discounted.
9. **Provide closure:** Ask the recipient to respond, then paraphrase their opinion and ask whether they have any questions. End by clearly stating behavioural expectations.

BE AWARE OF LANGUAGE PATTERNS

Listen to the language pattern of the person to whom you want to give feedback. We can give our feedback in rapport when we match the representational system of the other person. By doing this, they will be more predisposed to listen and take on board what we say. They will recognize that we are talking their language and understand our points. So how do we do this?

There are three main representational systems – **visual**, **auditory** and **kinaesthetic**. Although we use all three at various times, there will be one that is our natural default and that we feel more comfortable in. Listen to the words a person uses to find out their preferred system.

If they predominantly use **visual** language and use phrases such as 'Seeing things from their point of view…', 'Look at it this way', 'Can you picture how it will look?' and so on, then they are visual and your feedback will be better understood if you also use visual words and speak in images.

If they are **auditory** and talk a lot about 'hearing what you say', 'listening to all the arguments', 'talking about the pros and cons', then you can match this by doing the same. Auditory people are inclined to speak more slowly than visual people, so keep what you have to say measured and slow because they'll want to hear what you have to say.

Someone who is **kinaesthetic** will talk about 'getting the message' or 'getting to grips with the task', 'feeling the vibes', 'needing to action something'. They are familiar with actions and feelings rather than images and talking. For them, actions speak louder than words.

Feedback delivered as a sandwich, assertively and focusing on the behaviour, will enable the recipient to take the learning in a positive way, as well intentioned, as a gift designed to help them achieve greater success in their professional or personal life. The feedback sandwich is applicable in all walks of life and for all ages.

19 Give feedback without words

'This is an essential foundation of NLP: it is the structure we hold within that influences our perception and our feelings toward what we experience outside of ourselves.' Sue Knight

'You have to clearly distinguish between what you are getting from the outside and how you are interpreting that material in a complex manner at the unconscious level, contributing to it by your own internal state.' Richard Bandler and John Grinder

'Pay attention on the inside – don't be clumsy on the inside and you won't be clumsy on the outside. Succeed on the inside and you will succeed on the outside.' Joseph O'Connor

'Wisdom comes with the ability to be still. Just look and just listen. No more is needed.' T.K. Horne

'Children are educated by what the grown-up is and not by his talk.' Carl Jung

'Every word, facial expression, gesture, or action on the part of a parent gives the child some message about self-worth. It is sad that so many parents don't realize what messages they are sending.' Virginia Satir

In a world where silence is a rare commodity, it has soared in value. We walk around with our ear to a cellphone or iPod, conduct multiple conversations and are seldom unconnected to some device or another. Feedback comes in verbal and written form almost immediately, as colleagues, friends and family respond instantly to emails and texts. Thinking time to process what's been said or what has happened has been reduced to a microsecond. Yet, feedback is how we learn to do something different next time.

There is no failure, only feedback. When we do something we get a result. If that result is good, we use feedback to learn the structure of what we did well so we can build on it and repeat it even better next time. If the result is not so great, then we use feedback to work out what we could do differently next time. We are constantly learning and tweaking, like a gymnast walking along a beam, making minute adjustments constantly to maintain her balance. She may look down but usually she looks ahead, focusing on the end goal, the end of the beam.

Athletes use feedback all the time, listening for the sound of the ball bouncing on the racquet and the ground, the sound of the skis on the snow (or ice!), the wind in the sail and so on. Performers listen for laughter or lack of it, so they know what positive feedback sounds like.

Our body gives us feedback silently all the time. It tells us when we are tired and need to rest, when we've eaten enough food, when we are straining a muscle and when we are feeling unwell. In sport, it is particularly important to notice the impact on your body from different training routines and certain foods. Notice the subtle psychological shifts when you do a particular sport well and when you don't do it so well. Sense the level of relaxation in your shoulders after a good shot or the feeling in your stomach as you approach a conversion in rugby. Be aware of how your body feels when you are on the right track and keep it there.

If you are trying to lose weight, you'll see feedback every week on the scales and learn from how much you've lost whether you've been making the right choices. You'll also get feedback from your clothes as to how tight they feel, or how loose if you're doing well. A good way to use feedback when you are losing weight is to keep an exercise and food diary to record exactly what you are doing, so you learn what works and what doesn't.

Children look for feedback all the time, noting their parents' facial expressions and body language. They want to see smiles and hugs, and that's what they are aiming for, so the absence of them will tell your child that you are not pleased with their behaviour. You don't always have to say something. A stern look, a frown and the absence of a smile often tell your child as much as they need to know about what you think of their behaviour.

When we give feedback, we need to be aware that what we have observed may well also be true for us, not perhaps in exact detail but in essence. By not immediately speaking and instead thinking of how we, too, might exhibit the same behaviour we are able to consider what underlying belief we have that the other person may also have.

When you receive feedback, it can be tempting to launch into a detailed discussion; it can also be tempting to defend yourself if you think you are being criticized. Instead, though, next time you are given feedback, listen, smile and thank them for the feedback.

Feedback is a gift and it is being given for you to learn from it. So maintain eye contact as they give it and be curious about what they are saying and what the learning could be for you.

Ask questions to clarify but avoid explanations and excuses. 'Thank you' is enough.

BODY LANGUAGE

When giving or receiving feedback, pay attention to what your body is saying:

- Signs of being **defensive** or **angry** are: crossed arms and/or legs, clenched fists, tight jaw, overall stiffness and short breaths.
- Signs of **fear** and **anxiety** are: nail-biting, fidgeting, being unfocused, lack of eye contact.
- Signs of **embarrassment** are: lack of eye contact, blushing, hunched body posture, nervous laugh.
- Signs of **not connecting** are: avoiding people, lack of eye contact, monotonous voice, monosyllabic replies, tight mouth.

DEVELOP YOUR SENSITIVITY TO NON-VERBAL FEEDBACK

We can train ourselves to be more sensitive to unspoken feedback – to watch body language and listen for changes in voice tone. There is a tendency, with the increase in use of technology as a means of communication, to lose some of the subtlety of language as we reduce the characters to fit a Tweet or cut down words for speed in texting. We use emoticons to express our feelings and symbols for smiles and LOL for laughter. However, we are more sophisticated than this, and when communication is reduced to content, we lose the ability to express ourselves and understand other people. Face-to-face conversation enables us to appreciate facial gestures, shifts in body position, lapses in eye contact, and the pace, tone and pitch of the spoken word. It also enables us to match and establish the level of rapport we need for effective feedback. Where possible, give your feedback face, to face not via technology.

THE ABSENCE OF FEEDBACK

When we say nothing at all when feedback is expected, this can be construed by others as negative feedback – for example, when someone doesn't respond to an email or doesn't call you after a date. Many people would expect you to follow them if they have followed you on Twitter. There are lots of ways you can give negative feedback by not responding, so choose carefully when to speak and when not to, when to respond and when not to. In the space where no response is made the other person takes their feedback, so make sure they are going to get the learning without words. Sportspeople, for example, don't need you to tell them whether they made a good shot and most people know for themselves when they've done well. Not everyone needs verbal feedback.

Putting it all together

Before you even start to give feedback verbally, you are already communicating non-verbally, and research shows that this is the first thing we notice when we communicate. Be aware of this non-verbal communication, whether you are giving or receiving feedback, and ensure that it reflects what you intend. Your body is constantly communicating; mind and body are one, so use this as feedback. Although verbal feedback is valuable learning, be sure to make the most of the non-verbal feedback you give and receive.

20 Give feedback to your children

 'Having a two-year-old is like having a blender that you don't have the top for.' Jerry Seinfeld

 'Anyone who thinks the art of conversation is dead ought to tell a child to go to bed.' Robert Gallagher

'There's nothing that can help you understand your beliefs more than trying to explain them to an inquisitive child.' Frank A. Clark

'It is easier to build strong children than to repair broken men.' Frederick Douglass

'A child seldom needs a good talking to as a good listening to.' Robert Brault

As parents or teachers, carers of children, you have a very important role to play in giving them feedback. Feedback is a gift of love that shows you care about them and have an investment in their personal development. Can there be anything worse than being ignored? Children need to know that you're paying attention to them and they want to know where they need to make changes, because that's your job as a parent – to guide them so that they can achieve all they can in life.

The giving and receiving of feedback is how we learn. At its simplest level, a stand-up comedian will adapt his programme constantly to suit his audience with more of what they are clapping and cheering and less of what gets no reaction. We need to be a bit like the stand-up comedian and notice where we get a connection with our children when they do what we asked and are being resourceful. When they are not, we need to use feedback to get them back on track. We need to constantly be open and curious to what is working and getting a result – the result we want, anyway! We are getting feedback from them and giving them feedback; it is a constant flow of energy and learning.

Many people feel that they learn more from their mistakes than from successes. In fact, pupils who struggled with maths at school become excellent maths teachers because they understand how others get it wrong. As parents, we can be inclined to jump in and do things for our children, take responsibility for organizing them and their free time, and even decide when and where homework should be done. Allowing children to take responsibility from an early age means that they will make mistakes, and our job is to allow them to do that and let them get the learning so that the next time they do it, they do it better. Encourage them to be curious because that is how children learn, by wanting to know more and to understand rather than being told.

Feedback is how they learn – whether that is feedback in terms of a bad mark at school, losing a tennis match or football game, losing a friend, missing the bus, getting a detention for homework not completed correctly; these are all feedback from which they will learn how to improve and get a better result. When these sorts of things happen to children, let them get the feedback rather than believing that, unless you tell them, they won't know.

When we aren't introduced to feedback as learning, we can find ourselves taking it as criticism and becoming defensive, or we feel a failure and lose self-esteem. You can show your children how to respond to feedback by how you demonstrate it yourself. The best way to show them how to respond is to pause, be curious about the learning and thank the giver of the feedback.

ENCOURAGE CHILDREN TO GIVE THEMSELVES FEEDBACK

We all, even children, have a nagging little inner voice that gets cross and tells us off, but every child needs to learn how to give themselves feedback in a way that they can learn from, without feeling permanently stupid and losing confidence.

Get them to ask themselves the following:

1. What specifically went well today? (three things)
2. What could have been better? (one thing)
3. How could I do that better next time?
4. Overall, what lessons have I learned?

You can teach this to pre-school children upwards. Encourage them to 'read' feedback non-verbally, so ask them how they know something went well. What were the signs? Were they noticing what people said or how they looked or what they did?

We have a tendency to have a preference, whether visual, auditory or kinaesthetic, so if your child generally tends to notice people's visual response to them, encourage them to also listen to what is said and done, so that you can open their minds up to all three types of feedback.

CHILD-FRIENDLY FEEDBACK

Feedback to children needs to be:

1. **Immediate** – there's no point in spending days thinking about it and then expecting them to remember what they did. Children have very short memories and will have forgotten what they did, why they did it and wonder why you're talking about it days later.
2. **Specific** – you need to draw their attention to the specific thing they did or said and what exactly they need to do more of or less of, because they won't be able to read your mind. They need to know what you want from them.

3. **Sincere** – the feedback needs to reflect what you think and what you believe and be something they can see is of value to you. Use 'I' to show that it is what you think and don't bring other people into it. It doesn't matter what anyone else thinks. Keep this between you and your child.
4. **Short** – avoid long sentences and lengthy explanations about why you feel like this; it isn't helpful. Use the KISS principle – keep it simple, stupid.
5. **What you _do_ want** – avoid the word 'don't'; tell them instead what you want them to do – either more of something or less of something.
6. **Without the word 'but'** – because your positive start will be forgotten once you use the word 'but'. Replace it with the word 'and'.
7. **Accepting** – because you are not a mind-reader, so don't presume to know what their intentions were. Instead, give them the benefit of the doubt and look for their positive intention. For the most part, children want to please you, but their map of the world is different from yours with other more pressing priorities such as playing!
8. **Focused on the behaviour** rather than being a personal attack on their identity.

THE FEEDBACK SANDWICH FOR CHILDREN

Use the feedback sandwich with children. You can do this from the youngest age through to even grown-up children.

The feedback sandwich starts with making a **positive comment** about what you've observed that is good. You may need to be very observant here because sometimes when your child is being very naughty it can be hard to find anything positive. If you child is throwing a tantrum, you could comment on what a loud voice they have or how you notice they are good at attracting attention to themselves.

Your initial positive reponse can be non-verbal. You can smile or touch them to show you have a positive intention.

The next bite of the sandwich is the filling. This is the **main message** – the piece you want to communicate to them as learning. It could be something you'd like to see more of such as speed – if they're taking their time getting ready for school – or focus on homework – if they're watching TV – or consideration – if perhaps they're leaving mess around the house. It could be something you'd like less of such as noise, mess, answering back, playing video games and so on.

The filling of the sandwich needs to be delivered with a lower voice than you normally use – slower, more deliberate and with minimum words. Children's attention span is short, so keep the message to a minimum.

Finally, end on a **good note** and leave them with something to learn from but also feeling good about themselves. Mention how much you love them and want the best for them, that you're proud of them and think they're great.

Putting it all together

Give feedback to your children with love and focus on how they can learn from it and become the excellent human being you want them to be. Show them how to respond to feedback by demonstrating it and by being flexible about your choices of how to give and receive it – because sometimes feedback not given in a resourceful way can be demeaning and hurtful.

Manage your moods

❝ *'Change your physiology and you change your emotion. When I smile and you smile in return, that smile passes on happiness to you.'* Joseph O'Connor

'How well you learn depends on the state you are in. How well you perform depends on what state you are in. Whatever task you have to perform, whatever you want to learn, whatever outcome you want, ask yourself: "What state do I want to be in to make this easy?"' Joseph O'Connor

❝ *'Leading starts with the ability to lead ourselves. To do this we need first and foremost to be able to manage our emotional state. If we feel irritation, guilt, anger, frustration, doubt or self-consciousness, the result will be less than we are capable of and is unlikely to be a win/win. In contrast, feelings of ease, confidence, forgiveness, acceptance, inspiration and amusement are states that are much more likely to lead to us giving of our best, whatever the context.'* Sue Knight

'You have to realize that you can create any state you want whenever you want,. You can learn to look at the same piece of personal history in a different way because the truth is that it's not your personal history that makes you who you are, it's your response to it.' Richard Bandler

'Emotions make excellent servants, but tyrannical masters.'
John Seymour

A 'mood' is another word for our emotional state. These moods change over the course of the day and are affected both by external events and by what is going on in our head (internal events), our thoughts and feelings. Most people allow their state to determine their behaviour but, by understanding the process and its structure, we can learn how to take charge and manage our moods.

Managing your state is important for many reasons. At work, we cannot function effectively if we are at the mercy of unpredictable mood swings; our colleagues wouldn't know how to respond to us and we'd be unable to cope with pressure. It could certainly be a barrier to advancement. There are also serious mental and physical health consequences when we allow our emotional state to govern us. High blood pressure, risks of heart attacks, digestion problems and headaches, as well as depression and anxiety, can also result from the pressure of not being in control of our emotional state. Lastly, healthy relationships rely on the ability to control our emotional state so we can communicate well and express our feelings.

The NLP Communication Model (see Appendix) helps us to understand how our emotional state can be affected by external events. An external event is something that happens. This can be something we see, hear or experience. We process these differently depending on our map of the world, which is based on our memories, beliefs and values. Our map is unique to us, which explains why the same external event may stimulate different emotional states in other people. We then filter the event by making our own internal representation of it. We select what we take from it, omitting some parts of the event, generalizing other parts and distorting some parts of it until we have our own version of it. Now we have a state and it may not be one that is resourceful. A resourceful state is one that enables us to do what we have to do and do it well. An unresourceful state is the opposite and prevents us from being effective.

Here is an example: Jack has just been asked to explain his new product idea at a team meeting. Last time he did something like this, his manager found fault with it and Jack felt embarrassed and stupid. This reminded him of how he used to feel at school when he got an answer wrong in class. So, in his panic, his internal representation became distorted such that he now thinks everything he comes up with is stupid and he feels like a little boy again. That time, his head went down and he felt a bit sick, so much so that he had to leave the room and he then felt even worse and even more stupid. Can you see how Jack worked through the NLP Communication Model, from external event to behaviour?

HOW DO WE KNOW WHAT STATE WE ARE IN?

We need to know our baseline state as a benchmark so we can learn to recognize when we are in a different state. Our baseline state is long established and it's the state we are in when we are relaxed and comfortable with ourselves.

Let's calibrate it so we know how to recognize it, and from there we can learn to recognize other states that we may want to work on.

Do this now by becoming aware of your state. Check in with yourself for a moment – it may help to close your eyes. Let's work from the outside in. If you had a mirror to hand or could see yourself, how would you look? How is your body posture? Notice everything from your toes to the top of your head and make sure that you are comfortable (not lounging about, just resting nicely in a calm state). On a scale of 1–10, how tense is your body and is this the same in every part of your body? How high is your energy level?

Now go inside and become aware of how you feel right now. What adjectives would you use to describe how you're feeling? What skills are you conscious of right now? On a scale of 1–10, how happy do you feel in yourself? Do you have anything on your mind?

Take a mental snapshot of how you are now and file this as your baseline state.

NOW LET'S PLAY!

How would you like to have a play with your state?

In NLP, we consider the mind and the body to be one. They directly influence each other – if you play a sport, you will be very aware of this. Exercise is the best way to improve your mood as you change almost every part of your physiology and by focusing on the exercise and the external, you take your mind off internal thoughts and feelings.

So let's start with making a few changes to the outside and notice what that does inside. A quick and easy way of doing that is to write alongside each of the following instructions a score of 1–10 for your happiness level.

1. Smile.
2. Look up.
3. Laugh.
4. Frown.
5. Look down.
6. Sigh.
7. Stand up.
8. Jog on the spot.

Now for the inside – again, make a note alongside each point of how each one changes your happiness level. Also notice how your physiology changes.

1. Think about something sad.
2. Think about a happy moment.
3. Think about when you did a great piece of work of which you felt proud.
4. Think about when you were a child.
5. Recall a sporty success.

Have you discovered that changing the outside changes the inside, and vice versa? So now you know how to manage your state. You are responsible for your own state. Do not blame other people for how you choose to feel. It really is up to you. Some people use drugs and alcohol to change their state, or they buy themselves new things, phone friends hoping they will cheer them up, but when you know how to change your own state you are in control.

CONTAGIOUS STATES

The other interesting thing about states is that they can be contagious. People are attracted to other people in whose company they enjoy a resourceful state.

Use this knowledge to gain rapport and instantly make friends and influence people.

If you're with someone who is unhappy and you want to cheer them up, you can match their body language initially and match their language patterns. Sigh when they sigh and look upset when they do. Match their body posture and how they hold their head. Use similar words and you will soon find it easy to empathize with them. Then gradually mismatch – this is called 'pacing to lead'. You have been pacing them, but now start to change the body language a bit. Make it gradual. Start by encouraging them to look up – maybe notice something in the sky or in a tree. Looking up automatically raises the spirits.

If the pace of their voice has been quite slow, speed yours up a little. If it's been in a low tone, slightly raise yours. If you have both been very static, shift position. Be careful not to do everything at the same time, though, as you need to stay in rapport.

Add a little energy and move the focus on 'towards' and positive language, so that, instead of focusing on what they *don't* have (happiness), you notice what they *do* have. In no time, their spirits will have been lifted through the mind-and-body connection. You will have changed their state through pacing and leading.

Putting it all together

Managing moods or states starts with taking responsibility for your own and recognizing that it isn't up to other people to make you happy or to make you feel good about yourself. They also can't make you angry or sad. By changing your inner dialogue and your internal representation of the external event, and by changing your response through changing your physical behaviour, you can – through a series of checks and balances and, with your baseline state in mind – create for yourself the most resourceful state for you at that moment.

22 Anchor a great state

'Leading starts with the ability to lead ourselves. To do this we need first and foremost to be able to manage our emotional state.' Sue Knight

'How well you learn depends on the state you are in. How well you perform depends on what state you are in. Whatever task you have to perform, whatever you want to learn, whatever outcome you want, ask yourself: "What state do I want to be in to make this easy?"' Joseph O'Connor

'Anchoring, and the construction of new possibilities using anchoring, can literally convert your personal history from a set of limitations to a set of resources.' Richard Bandler and John Grinder

'You have to realize that you can create any state you want whenever you want.' Tony Robbins

'To believe that someone else is responsible for your emotional state is to give them a sort of psychic power over you they do not have ... we really do generate our own feelings. No one else can do it for us. We respond and are responsible. To think other people are responsible for our feelings is to inhabit a billiard ball, inanimate universe.' John Seymour

Imagine if you could, by using a simple action, immediately transport yourself into a great state that was exactly the one you needed for that moment. Yes, it really is possible. You have the resources to do whatever you want. All you need to be able to do is remember the feeling you want so you need to have had that feeling before or something like it.

Anchoring is about associating. Do you remember learning about Pavlov's dogs at school? Ivan Pavlov was a psychologist working in the early 1900s. He was experimenting with unconditioned responses with dogs by measuring the dogs' salivation when they were presented with a bowl of food. What he found, though, was that the dogs also salivated when they saw the lab assistants because they had learned to associate them with food. This was not an unconditioned response; the dogs had learned to make the association. Pavlov further developed this work by replacing the lab assistants with a bell and he sounded the bell just before he gave the dogs their food. After a few times, the same result occurred as the dogs learned to associate the bell with food. This is called a **conditioned response**. Later this was developed by John Watson, who defined **classical conditioning** as learning to associate an unconditioned stimulus that already brings about a particular response or reflex with a new conditioned stimulus so that the new stimulus brings about the same response. This is what anchoring is: we are learning a new response to replace the unwanted one.

You probably recognize that humans have some unconditioned responses. These are things like feeling hungry when we smell food, smiling when we see a child doing something cute, laughing at a joke, crying when we peel onions. We haven't learned these responses; they just happen naturally. These aren't bad or negative responses, but sometimes we do have responses we'd rather not have, such as tensing up and being unable to speak when the corporate CEO approaches us or stammering when a pretty girl or an attractive man catches our eye. Some people's reaction to spiders, mice and dogs can be very awkward.

In life, we do sometimes have to do things that we find frightening, embarrassing, painful or upsetting in some way, so we need a resource that will enable us to associate into a better, more resourceful state, where we can cope with whatever it is that worries us. As small children we probably had a favourite teddy bear or we gripped our mum's hand really tightly or perhaps we were bribed with sweeties! As grown-ups, though, we are expected to do more and to do it on our own, so we need a resource that is ours and that is something we have wherever we go.

FIND THE STATE WITHIN YOU...

First, we need to establish what **state** you need. A state is a mood or way of being, such as brave, confident, desirable, fast, strong and so on, depending on the context. For example, a golfer might need feelings of calm before taking a golf shot, power for the drive, care for the put and so on. Being able to identify what you need and at what point is the first part of the exercise in anchoring.

So think about a situation where you don't feel comfortable. Maybe it's something that brings on a negative reaction or something you find frightening.

Now think about what reaction you'd like to have instead of the one you usually have. Picture yourself having that reaction and listen to what you're saying, watch what you are doing. What's the state you have in this desired outcome? Give it a name.

Now, when do you usually have this state? Somewhere in your life you have experienced this state and have access to it. Remember, we have all the resources we need. So bring it to mind and associate into it. This means to relive it as if it's happening right now. Does it match what you imagined before? Will this state work for you in the situation you need it for? If the answer is 'yes', then you're ready to start anchoring. If 'no', then think again about when you had the state you will need. It may have been in the past. It may have been in a sport, socially, at work, at home or on holiday.

Ask your family and friends or your colleagues, 'When have you known me to be X?' – maybe they have observed a state that you were not aware of. Sometimes we take states for granted, especially if we are used to them. If, say, you always feel relaxed when you are with your friend and need to access a relaxed state, you may not think of this if it's always been so.

FIND YOUR ANCHOR…

Now you're ready to **anchor**, but what shall we use as an anchor? We need the equivalent of the bell in Pavlov's experiment. Of course, we can't go around ringing bells when we want to conjure up our desired state. We need a subtle action or sign.

Some people like to use a discreet 'thumbs-up' or 'OK' sign. Others prefer to squeeze their earlobe. You must choose an action that you can do easily and discreetly anywhere.

If you are **visual** and pay attention to what you see, then a good anchor for you might be wearing something that you can associate with the state. Perhaps you'd prefer to think of a picture in your head that reminds you of the state.

If you are **auditory**, then a sound might work well for you. You might have a word you say to yourself, or a phrase that fires you and gives you the state you want. There may be a piece of music that puts you in the mood you want and you could hum it; some people put it on their phone or iPod. Runners, for example, select tracks that will set a good pace.

Kinaesthetic people tend to prefer an action as an anchor. They will decide on something like touching a piece of jewellery, or patting a part of their body, or putting their thumb and first finger together to form an 'O'.

Once you've discovered anchoring, you'll want to have different anchors for different states, so be prepared to have several. Make sure that you know what anchors which state, though!

ANCHOR!

Are you ready to anchor now? You've got the state you want and you have the anchor, so let's start.

Take yourself somewhere quiet to learn this technique because, although you will need to be able to use your anchor anywhere, when you first set it up you need peace and quiet.

1. Close your eyes and think about the state you want to anchor. Put yourself in the place, get the feeling,

hear the sounds, see what's around you, see yourself, feel the feelings and get the actions. This is called **associating**. When the experience is rich and vibrant, apply your anchor.

2. Hold it there until the experience dims slightly and, when it does, remove your anchor and give yourself a little shake to 'break state'.

3. Repeat the exercise again, doing exactly the same thing. You can change the experience a little if you like, but make sure you're anchoring exactly the same state even if it's in a different situation.

4. Do it a third time and keep doing it until you automatically get the state when you use your anchor. You'll need to practise it quite a bit to begin with until it becomes a learned response. You can then use it as the desired response to get the desired state whenever you need it.

Putting it all together

Our state affects how we are, how we learn and how we play, how we are with others and how we feel about ourselves. It is up to us to ensure that it is something we can control; otherwise we are at the mercy of those around us. We need to take responsibility for it, constantly calibrate (check it) and, when we find it wanting, make adjustments by anchoring the state we need.

23 Be aware of unconscious anchors

> 'Recognising an anchor will not neccessarily neutralize it but it will weaken its power.' Reg Connolly

> 'Anchoring, and the construction of new possibilities can literally convert your personal history from a set of limitations to a set of resources.' Richard Bandler and John Grinder

> 'The ability to choose the best emotional state to suit your circumstances is one of the most powerful and yet most overlooked skills you can have.' Sue Knight

> 'To have control over our frame of mind at any given point is a great asset in determining the success and enjoyment of our day-to-day lives.' Jeff Archer

> 'Anchors are everywhere. Have you ever been in a classroom where there's a blackboard and somebody went up to the blackboard and went (he pantomimes scraping his fingernails down the blackboard. Most people wince or groan). What are you doing? You're crazy. There's no blackboard. How's that for an anchor?' Richard Bandler and John Grinder

An **anchor** is the NLP name for a trigger or stimulus that calls forth an emotional response in us such as a state of being brave or calm or, indeed, whatever we choose to anchor. As we saw in Chapter 22, the process of anchoring was developed from work done by the scientist Ivan Pavlov who discovered that his dogs had so strongly associated the sound of a bell with being fed that they responded to it as though they were about to be fed, even when no food was forthcoming. We use this principle in NLP to create states that will be resourceful to us by creating an anchor for them consciously. But unconscious anchors already exist for each one of us. Do you recognize yours?

An **unconscious anchor** is the sight, sound or feel of something that unconsciously triggers a memory, experience or a feeling in us that is either resourceful or unresourceful. A resourceful trigger is when this unconscious anchor creates a good feeling in us or provokes good performance, such as when we're driving on the motorway and catch sight of a splash of yellow stripe and (unconsciously), thinking it could be a police car, we slow down to the speed limit (or just under). An unresourceful anchor triggers something negative or a bad performance – for example, if we go to a job interview and the interviewer reminds us of someone who bullied us at school, we perform badly and don't get the job.

In NLP, the 'P' stands for programming and this is the word we give for the habits and programmes we run in our lives. Anchors are what we respond to unconsciously and we tend to respond the same way again and again, even though it may not be helpful. What if we could bring unconscious anchors to our conscious awareness and we could then control the result we get? We can do this in two ways. We could override the unresourceful anchor with a positive one, or we could use a technique called the **SWISH**.

To replace the negative troublesome anchor with a resourceful one, identify the response you would like to have and associate into it by imagining you are experiencing it now. As you do this and when the feeling is at its most intense, squeeze your earlobe. This is the new conscious anchor. Do this a few times to establish it and then imagine yourself doing this the next time you experience the trigger.

USE THE SWISH TECHNIQUE

To SWISH, imagine you are watching a TV and on it is a picture of you having a negative reaction to something. Because your trigger is unconscious, you might not even know what the reaction is all about; you just know you are not in a resourceful state and you are not sure why. What you do know is that you need to change it to a resourceful one, whether that is upbeat, calm or happy. In the bottom right-hand side of the screen, place an image of you in that desired state. Now sweep your hand across in front of you as if swatting a fly and, as you do that, make the unresourceful picture go into the right-hand corner and bring the resourceful image to the centre of the screen. Do this several times and make sure you can do it at will. Now, whenever you sense that something has triggered a negative reaction in you, SWISH it away and replace it with a good one.

IDENTIFY UNCONSCIOUS TRIGGERS

Unconscious visual anchors can be an old photograph that triggers memories of your childhood and perhaps people no longer with you. Perhaps the photograph reminds you of your family home, a wonderful holiday, you when you were younger. Photographs trigger unconscious emotions because we cannot control them. However, we could *consciously* use an old photograph as an anchor if we wanted to create that feeling whenever we wished.

The sight of a friend across the street or in a crowd, unexpected, can be a joyful trigger, as can the sight of your child on stage at their first school play or in their wedding dress.

There can be negative visual triggers, too. The sight of an untidy room springs to mind, as do plates left on the table or dirty clothes left on the floor, which can trigger annoyance in most parents of teenagers.

The sight of a bill, your bank statement or a letter from someone you don't want to hear from can create a sense of panic.

What visual triggers create an unconscious reaction in you?

UNCONSCIOUS AUDITORY ANCHORS

Unconscious auditory anchors can be the sound of someone's voice or a piece of music, or the scratching of chalk on a blackboard, which can be unpleasant to some people. The sound of post landing on the doormat, the sound of a dog barking, a gate squeaking, a text message beeping, a phone going off in the theatre or papers rustling – all these can be anchors.

Music can be very evocative and music from your childhood or teen life can conjure up a plethora of happy memories.

The sound of someone's voice can work as an unconscious anchor depending on whether it has pleasant or unpleasant associations, and you may find that, if someone you meet sounds like someone you used to know, you will unconsciously associate their voice with that person.

A newborn baby's cry will melt the heart of every mother in a supermarket, just as the sound of a small child's tantrum will make them smile as they recall their own embarrassments.

For sports fans, the sound of a cricket ball being hit for a six, an ace service or the roar of racing cars round a track will send the adrenalin rushing.

KINAESTHETIC UNCONSCIOUS ANCHORS

Kinaesthetic unconscious anchors can be the touch of your partner, your child's hand in yours, stroking Grandma's wrinkled hand or touching a baby's cheek.

Be aware of when you touch your partner and what unconscious anchors you might be setting up. Well-established couples often touch each other only when they feel bad and need a hug; your touch is anchored to bad feelings unconsciously in just the same way as if you only touch each other when you are making love. Touch each other when you feel happy and you'll have a positive unconscious anchor which will cheer you up when you feel sad.

It is well known how the touch of a hand on dog's fur can work at an unconscious level for stroke patients, severely disabled people and those in a coma. It is known to reduce the heart rate and aid recovery. Therapy dogs go into schools for children to stroke them as they read – this has been found to reduce stuttering and stammering, increase confidence and aid fluency.

Different textures can evoke emotional feelings, prompt memories and have positive or negative effects at a subconscious level.

Putting it all together

Next time you find yourself responding in a way that surprises you or disappoints you and you realize that it isn't the most helpful state, it is probably an unconscious anchor that has been triggered. Take action immediately and use your conscious anchor or use the SWISH to remove it.

24 Use anchoring to relieve stress

'The greatest weapon against stress is our ability to choose one thought over another.' William James

'The truth is that stress doesn't come from your boss, your kids, your spouse, traffic jams, health challenges or other circumstances. It comes from your thoughts about these circumstances.' Andrew Bernstein

'Stress is the trash of modern life – we all generate it but if you don't dispose of it properly, it will pile up and overtake your life.' Terri Guillemets

'Life is not what it's supposed to be. It's what it is. The way you cope with it is what makes the difference.' Virginia Satir

'Persistent stress, for example, may be reduced by identifying bodily tensions; by evoking awareness of the feelings that fuel overwork; by uncovering mental attitudes such as perfectionism. It may be necessary to work on all three separately.' John Whitmore

Anchoring is a self-hypnosis technique that can be used to bring about a conscious association between an action, image or sound and a desired state. We all have unconscious anchors, we respond with stress when faced with particular challenges and conscious anchoring can be used to override that unconscious reaction with a more resourceful one.

Stress is a reaction to a situation and it is different in all of us. While most of us thrive under a certain amount of pressure – indeed, we often find it exciting – there comes a point when our response to it is no longer resourceful. It is extremely useful to be able to recognize when you are approaching this ineffective point so that you can manage the situation to avoid the onset of stress. Check in with yourself regularly – by this, we mean just stop for a moment and take a few deep breaths. Ask yourself whether you are in control or is the situation in control of you? What could you do to take back control?

In some situations, we may have an unconscious stress response to certain situations such as your teenager asking to be picked up late from a party or your boss asking you to work late (those are both auditory stimuli). You could react with stress on seeing a queue at the checkout or seeing your name down for the late shift at work (visual stimuli), or you may react more to kinaesthetic stimuli such as someone jogging you as they rush past or finding you can't do up your trousers. How do you respond in these situations? Do you respond more to one type than another, perhaps? What causes you stress will be different from what causes it in other people.

The previous two chapters cited the work of Ivan Pavlov, who discovered when he experimented with feeding his dogs that they responded by salivating when he fed them, which is not too surprising. He decided to ring a bell at the same time as he fed them, which led the dogs to associate the bell sounding with food. They continued to respond by salivating when the bell sounded even when food was not offered because they had learned to associate the bell with food. This is how **anchoring** works. We train our body to respond to an action, like the sound of the bell, in a particular way. We can then use this as an anchor, to make ourselves respond in this new desired way instead of in the way we don't want. We wouldn't want to go around ringing bells, so instead we choose a more discreet anchor such as squeezing our thumb and forefinger together. In this way, we can replace our unwanted response of stress with a response we do want.

We need to decide what we do want if we don't want stress; after all, it's difficult to focus on what we don't want because that's exactly what we're likely to get. Once we have identified our desired state in our mind, we need to associate into it. What that means is imagining that we are experiencing it right now. So close your eyes and imagine it and, when it is really strong, use the anchor you have chosen and hold it there while you are truly associated into the feeling. As it ebbs away, take away your anchor as well. Break state by giving yourself a little shake and repeat the process three times to really strengthen the association between the anchor and the associated feeling.

VISUAL, AUDITORY OR KINAESTHETIC ANCHORS

If you are someone who thinks **visually** and notices what they see, then you might like to use a visual anchor. What that means is that, instead of making an action with your finger and thumb, you could imagine a scene that, immediately you picture it, takes away that stress. Perhaps it's somewhere you've been on holiday, a favourite place or a painting? You could even capture it as a screensaver or wallpaper on your phone so you have instant access to it.

If you are **auditory** and enjoy music, notice what you hear and are influenced by the sounds around you. then an auditory anchor may work well for you. You could record a favourite piece of music on your phone or iPod so you can listen to it when you feel stressed or hum it. Some auditory people like to use a specific word that resonates with them. You may find that just telling yourself to 'calm down' will be enough, if you're auditory.

A **kinaesthetic** person will probably be fine using a 'thumbs-up' sign, thumb and finger, or squeezing the earlobe. If you're a sportsperson, you may want to use a sports-related anchor such as bouncing the tennis ball a certain number of times before serving or touching part of the golf club, or something similar in your sport.

HOW TO RECOGNIZE STRESS

You need to know when to use your anchor and, ideally, it should be at the first sign of stress – not when it's well established.

Signs of stress are:

- you find it difficult to get to sleep and are still tired when you have to get up
- you find yourself getting snappy for no reason
- you keep getting colds or seem to be off work more than usual
- you have difficulty concentrating
- you find yourself making silly decisions or prioritizing the wrong things.

When you recognize any or several of these signs, accept them as signs of stress. This is feedback. Your body is telling you that you need to do something different, make a change. You have a choice. You can ignore the feedback and become more stressed, or you could use your anchor to relieve it.

ANCHOR A POSITIVE STATE

Currently you are responding to something by getting stressed. You may feel it in a specific part of your body. For example, some people get stress headaches, indigestion or skin reactions. Or you may react by stammering or finding it difficult to speak. What we need is an alternative response, one that will enable you to manage your state and do whatever it is that you need to do at that time.

Think about the situation that you dread. It may help to look up and to the left which is where we hold our visual memories.

Now look across and to the right and think instead about how you'd like to react instead. Perhaps you do sometimes react like that or have in the past? Visualize yourself reacting the way you'd like to act. How are you standing or sitting? What are you saying and how are you speaking? You can't control how others will react, but when you think about how you will be in your vision, assume that others will respond positively.

Now give this state a name. You might call it 'being brave' or 'confidence' or whatever your desired state is for you. Now you know what it is you want to anchor.

Putting it all together

Stress is a response to a situation that is no longer resourceful. While initially pressure might cause us to 'up our game' in response to it, further pressure can tip us over into a stressed state. Recognizing this tipping point is very important for managing our state and knowing at what point to use our anchor to create a resourceful state where we are in control.

25 Use anchoring for sport

'Sports people can often get themselves into 'A right state' before or during a big match or event. It is far more useful to be in "THE right state".' Jeremy Lazarus

'This can be done for all players. It can be done for the whole team. Do you think Harry Redknapp miraculously saved Portsmouth from certain relegation in 2004 by telling them about all their bad performances? He did not. He called them "fantastic", every time he could. He reminded players how good they were. That is anchoring. That is coaching. And that is motivation.' Ray Power

'The fight is won or lost far away from witnesses – behind the lines, in the gym, and out there on the road, long before I dance under those lights.' Muhammad Ali

'They can because they think they can.' Virgil

'Is it possible to think yourself into becoming a better rider? Yes, it is because all behavior is the result of neurological patterns. If a neurological pattern occurs, then the behavior occurs. By standing up to your fears, you can then disassociate yourself and install new positive images and mindsets to replace the disempowering images that imprison you.' Dr Lisa Christiensen

Anchoring is a technique for managing state. While arguably we might all want this technique as part of our skill set, sportspeople need it in order to ensure that they can control their performance. Imagine having an attack of nerves just before a big match or being distracted just as you need to make a crucial put. Sportsmen and women need a whole range of states at their disposal over the course of an event or training. Anchoring is the way they access these states.

DEVELOP YOUR ANCHOR(S) FOR SPORT

Here's how to anchor for sport. First, find a quiet place to do this exercise because you need to establish your anchor before you need to use it rather than when you are already feeling anxious or stressed. Decide on what you want your anchor to be. The anchor is the thing that you will think of to remind yourself of the state you want to be in. We set up an association between the anchor and the state so that, when you use the anchor, you get the state. It can be an image in your head, words you say to yourself, an action such as squeezing your earlobe or a 'thumbs-up' sign. Once you've decided what it will be, do it a few times so it becomes a natural movement. Remember that you'll need to use your anchor while you're playing your sport, so make sure it will be possible. For example, if you are a right-handed tennis player you need to use your left hand for the anchor action.

Now think about that great experience, the time you played sensationally well, the time everything came together in your performance. Get into that state by seeing it in your mind and hearing the sounds, seeing what you were seeing then, feeling everything you felt. When you are really in the state, use your anchor. Keep it there – whether it's a picture in your mind, a word you're saying or an action – until the feeling of being in that state subsides. When it does, take away the anchor because you only want the anchor in place when you are in the state – so that only the strongest positive state is associated with the anchor.

It's a good idea to 'break state' after doing this. That means you get up, walk around a bit and relax – it can be quite intense when you're conjuring up the experience and anchoring it when you are first learning to do it. Repeat this a couple of times using other examples and experiences of great shots, great serves, hits, drives or whatever your sport needs, each time using the anchor at the strongest point.

The best way to test that the anchoring is working is to use it! It could be that you need different states for different aspects of your game or sport, so you'll need to find different anchors for each. After all, the state you want for tackling in rugby is likely to be different than for scoring a conversion or a try and the same would be true for other sports. Remember how Jonny Wilkinson, for example, adopted a particular stance before he took a penalty kick. He knew that when he did this he would get his kicks on target.

POSITIVE AND NEGATIVE

In sport, you can anchor thoughts in players by reminding them of past experiences – a particular game, save, dribble or training session when they excelled. Sports coaches have the power and influence to create positive anchors, but equally they can unwittingly create negative ones, just as you can for yourself.

Reminding yourself of missed penalties, poor tackles or misplaced passes can ruin an otherwise successful performance. For example, if you remember that last time you played Team X you missed a crucial goal or you missed a pass, you have anchored the team negatively and will find it hard to overcome this unconscious anchor.

Instead of dwelling on negative performance, use anchoring to turn your performance around. Anchor that great save, that amazing goal, that fabulous pass.

You can build up some great experiences as you play by noticing the good strokes or the good passes and shots; as you do something well, log it for later when you can use it with your anchor. In this way you make your anchor stronger, so that when you need to use it you have a huge store of great experiences backing it up.

Some players have 'lucky' charms, something special they wear or something they do before they go on court. They may have a lucky mascot in their bag or someone special among the spectators who is their 'lucky' charm. These are all unconscious anchors. By performing a conscious anchoring process, we do away with luck and equip ourselves with something we have access to wherever we are and that isn't dependent on something or someone else.

VISUAL, AUDITORY, KINAESTHETIC

If you are **visual**, you may want to anchor an image such as receiving a medal or an award for your performance, the time you completed a winning race or the sight of your ball going in the hole. When you think visually, you will be more inspired and motivated by a visual anchor. Some people capture this with photographs, which they have on their mobile so they can flick through them before a competition. You can also use visual anchors during your game or performance – for example, you may find it easier to climb a hill on your bike when you just focus on the front wheel rather than the brow of the hill. A golfer who focuses on the back edge of the golf ball until the moment the club head strikes the ball will usually hit a better shot than the golfer who takes their eye off the ball earlier. When you do that your head rotates, which affects the resultnt shot by altering the balance of your body.

If you are **auditory**, you may prefer to use specific words to motivate you or a piece of music that you can hum. Again, you can put this on your mobile or iPod so it is accessible to you wherever you are. Many sportspeople unconsciously anchor with a sound based on that of the ball on their racquet or bat. They know how a good shot sounds and can even tell from the sound on the other person's racquet where their shot will go. You can amplify the sound and anchor by saying to yourself, 'Good shot' or 'Good ball.' When cycling or riding, become aware of what good performance sounds like and anchor it whenever you hear it, so that when you need to get into the state you can apply the anchor. Lots of teams have a team chant that they do before a game – this, again, is a conscious anchor.

Lots of sportspeople are **kinaesthetic** – they enjoy being active and they are conscious of the feelings in their body. Are they aware, though, of how they can use their body to create a state in their mind to improve performance? This is what anchoring is. By making a conscious action with our physiology we create a mental feeling that in turn will affect how we physically perform. Increase your awareness of your body stance – how does your body feel when it is performing at its most effective? Focus on breathing and controlling it to produce a calm state or an energetic, competitive state. Notice other people's physiology – what does that tell you about *their* state? Knowing when your opponent may be panicking or feeling vulnerable could open up a competitive advantage for you.

Putting it all together

Anchoring enables us to consciously associate a great resourceful state using an action, image or sound that we can apply whenever we need the state. This can overcome our unconscious negative anchors that get in the way of sports success and affect our state and performance. Mind and body are one. By increasing our awareness of how each affects the other, we increase our control and manage our behaviour by giving ourselves choices and flexibility. The person with the most flexibility controls the system.

26

Access the inner CCTV camera

> 'What people say they do or believe they do is often far removed from what they actually do.' Richard Bandler

> 'Wisdom comes from multiple perspectives, and there is a lot that the athlete can learn from seeing him/herself doing the particular event (disassociated) from different angles and perspectives.' Jeremy Lazarus

> 'The skill lies in choosing an associated or a disassociated state for a purpose. The appropriate choice depends on your desire outcome. You might choose to disassociate to protect yourself from painful emotions, or you might choose to associate in order fully to experience all the feelings of the situation.' Sue Knight

> 'As you practice the technique of changing perceptual positions you will find that moving to third position brings with it a new perspective and calmer insights into any dilemma that you are facing.' Jeff Archer

> 'Some people believe that this perceptual position allows us to manage our emotions more effectively by ensuring that our prefrontal cortex is engaged in a logical and rational way, as opposed to being at the mercy of our amygdala with all the associated risks of emotional excess.' Richard Churches and Roger Terry

Everything we experience is filtered through our beliefs and values, experiences and memories. This gives us a unique perception, ours. It is called our 'map of the world'. But there are several different ways of looking at our world. In NLP, we call them **positions**, or **perspectives**. They relate to perceptions from three different points of view. A CCTV camera has no emotion but simply records what it sees without judgement. It notices everything and records it exactly. It can't be fooled; it is impartial. By being able to access this state for ourselves we get to see what is actually happening in our world when we take away the emotions. This can be instructive in a number of situations.

First position is us. When we use the word 'I', we are engaging with our 'first person'. It is from this position that we think and talk about our thoughts and feelings, our beliefs and values, our experiences and our window on the world. It is important to associate into this position and be fully aware of it so you know that it is your opinion you are expressing and your choice to do what you are doing. You can't always stay in first position, though, because you need to appreciate other people's point of view and consider their feelings. Be aware when you are in first position and acknowledge that it is one point of view and that it isn't the only one.

Second position is the other person you are talking to or in a relationship with. You need to step into their shoes to understand the world from their perspective. It will be different from yours, not least because they may be another gender, age or ethnic group. You will be most successful at this if you can imagine and be curious about what life would be like if you were them. Acknowledging the second position is the way you can empathize with someone else and consider their feelings – by putting yourself in their shoes, you will know what these are without having to ask them.

Third position is the CCTV camera or, as some people say, 'the fly on the wall' or 'impartial observer'. This third position can observe what is going on between first and second position but cannot intervene and cannot feel the emotion; it just observes the body language and hears what is said. It can only communicate this without there being any judgement or emotion. In order to understand this position, imagine yourself as a CCTV camera watching you right now as you read this book. When you are that camera, what do you see? What is happening?

This ability to see things dispassionately can be enormously beneficial when emotions are getting high – being able to get into the second and third position in order to see the other person's map and see what is going on between you both from an outside perspective can take the heat out of the situation.

SWITCHING POSITIONS IN RELATIONSHIPS

Close relationships involve emotion; that's what marks them out as relationships rather than acquaintances. It means that what we say can hurt just as it can touch and give joy and love.

When you find yourself saying 'I feel...', 'I think...', 'You don't...', this is all first position and shows that you are totally associated into your own feelings. It's very unlikely that you will resolve your issue from this place. It will at best result in a compromise where each of you agrees to give in on something. This is a lose-lose situation in negotiation terms, as neither of you is actually very satisfied with what has been agreed.

Next time, move into third position and pretend you are a CCTV camera hovering above you both. From that disassociated place, look at the two of you – what do you see? Look at your expressions and your body language. Are you matching or mismatching? Listen to how you are both talking – how do you sound? Who is talking more loudly, who is talking faster, how is this affecting the interaction? What is being said? What words are they using?

Once you've observed for a while in third position, think about what you've seen and heard – what advice would you give first position (that's you)?

Now go back to first position and put that into action. Notice the difference as you match for rapport and become more aware of second position, having witnessed it from third position in an unemotional, observational way. You should now be able to negotiate a win-win.

USE YOUR CCTV CAMERA IN SPORT

Another situation in which this ability to observe dispassionately can be very useful is in sport. When you are fully associated, you notice all the feelings and experience disappointments when you lose a point or miss a pass. You also experience the highs of good shots and goals. But these highs and lows can create an emotionally exhausting experience where you miss out on the learning. One of the reasons coaches video sports performers is to show them what they are doing at all times during the game. Imagine if you could get that learning for yourself.

When you move into third position, you can observe what you are doing well and what needs work. You can effectively act as your own coach. This is called associated visualization. It enables you to experience the fullness of the event – what you see, hear, feel and even taste and smell. It is also a form of training for the body because there is research evidence to show that doing associated visualization stimulates the micro-muscles that link to the actual muscles that will be doing the sport.

DIET AND THE THIRD POSITION

If you're trying to lose weight, using this third position can be your ally. Imagine you are faced with your favourite cake, that glass of chilled white wine, whatever you might turn to after a long and stressful day at work. In first position you want it badly – you tell yourself you deserve a treat and this one looks so desirable. You know that it isn't part of your healthy eating plan but you'll go back to that tomorrow. Now you just want some comfort.

Maybe you even have a second position encouraging you – a friend or partner is having one and says, 'Come on, you deserve one after the day you've had.'

Instead, stop and move to third position. Move out of your body for a moment and see yourself looking at the cake or the glass of wine. From here you will see clearly what's happening and you won't feel the desire for the food because you'll be aware only of what you can see without those emotions getting in the way. As an observer, you see the cake or the wine quite differently and recognize that it doesn't belong in a healthy lifestyle. From this position you can suggest something else to first position (you) and tell them that they don't need this food and that they'll regret having it later. You can remind them that they'll feel better about themselves when they make a healthy choice. Third position allows you to see the best mutual solution rather than simply what suits you best (first position).

Putting it all together

Become aware of when you are in first, second and third position and practise moving deftly between them, to check out what the other person may need or want (second position), what you want (first position) and then check in with third position to view the interaction from a disassociated place where the emotions are quietened. That way, you become flexible, give yourself choices and are more likely to achieve your desirable outcome.

27

Look at the world from second position

> 'Before you criticize someone, walk a mile in his shoes.' Unknown

> 'By adopting second position we obtain important new information about our relationship with the other person. We're able to develop empathy and compassion for them. We also gather useful data about ourselves in the process. In our mind's eye we can look at ourselves, see our own facial expressions, add body language, hear our voice, and get a sense of what it's like to be on the receiving end of our own behaviour. This means we have increased choice about how to interact with them, which is especially useful when we can't understand why they are behaving the way they are.' Steve Bavister and Amanda Vickers

> 'One of the key reasons why there is conflict is because both people are stuck in their own mindset i.e. stuck in position 1. By one person changing their mindset towards the other person, the system will change. If one person stops being locked in his or her thinking, it is almost inevitable that the other person will change.' Jeremy Lazarus

> 'When you are fully in the other person's shoes and have their perspective on the situation, you are able to understand their map of the world. No matter how bizarre someone's behaviour might have seemed from your own perspective, in their shoes it is normal and perfectly understandable. To put ourselves fully into the shoes of another person allows us to tap into the emotions behind what they are doing and saying.' Sue Knight

Second position is that of the other person. You are the first person and the uninvolved bystander is the third person. Putting yourself in second position means stepping into the other person's shoes. It is all about empathy and building strong interdependent relationships. In this chapter, we will therefore be focusing on romantic relationships.

When we go into a relationship, we may not even notice how we are viewing our world because we are in love and, as we all know, love is blind. In the sense that much of how we communicate is unconscious, then it is blind. We do things without thinking because we want to please the other person with little thought about our own needs. We even watch things we wouldn't usually watch on TV, befriend their mum, spend time getting to know their friends and take hours getting ready for a date. This is being externally referenced. We care what they think of us so we guess what will please them. We may get it right or we may not. It isn't usually based on actually listening to them or second-positioning because we are still in those early stages of romance when we don't really pay attention to the detail, just to that lovely sense of being in love. We are in love with love, really.

Second position is different from being externally referenced because it is about really listening and watching and stepping into the other person's shoes. It's about being them, and by doing this you will really understand what they need from you and what's important to them because it will not just be based on what they say or ask but on what you experience. A good moment to put yourself into their shoes is when they do something that you usually find annoying. Instead of just thinking about what you find annoying – this is first position – step into their shoes and imagine finding it annoying for yourself. Be curious – what about it is annoying now that you're experiencing it? How important is it for you to do this thing in that way – could you find another way of doing it that isn't annoying? In everyday life, especially when we've been in a relationship for a long time and the initial infatuation and blindness have worn off, we can find all manner of things annoying in our partner, but when you step into their shoes and find it annoying for yourself, do you have another angle on it and can you find another way that isn't annoying?

When we put ourselves into second position we can enhance the experience by doing a physical exercise. Take three chairs and place them to form a triangle – they are what we call **spatial anchors** so we know who we are in each position. Sit in one – this is your chair and represents first position, where you speak as yourself. Direct your attention to another chair and call that second position – this is your partner. The third chair is the 'fly on the wall'. For now, speak to second position and express your thoughts and feelings about the issue that's concerning you. Then, when you're done, sit in the second-position chair and be your partner responding; it is important that you really associate into being your partner rather than simply mind-reading from first position. Really imagine that you are them and say what you have to say in response. You can switch chairs as often as you like as you gain clarity. Finally, sit in the third chair and comment on what you've noticed as a third-party observer.

SECOND-POSITION YOUR PARTNER

To second-position your partner, pay close attention to what they say, listening not for content but words that will tell you whether they are visual, auditory or kinaesthetic. Do they refer to what they've seen, heard or done? Do they ask you whom you've seen today, whom you've spoken to or what you've done? Do they notice what you look like? They could be **visual**. Do they enjoy a good chat? They could be **auditory**. If they're active, fidgety and enjoy playing sport, then they could be **kinaesthetic**. These are all rather basic definitions but should be enough to get you started in thinking which they are. Use the same language when you respond to them and notice the difference.

Notice whether they talk in detail (**small chunk**) or more big picture (**big chunk**) and use the same amount of detail when you talk to them. If they tend to focus on what they don't want rather than what they do want, match them and do the same. By matching, you are able to step into their shoes and experience what the world is like as them. Do they tend to agree or disagree? Someone who says 'Yes, but…' is mismatching, so do the same yourself and feel what it's like to be noticing what is wrong. By doing this, you will be in rapport and you will also be experiencing their way of processing. Maybe it will give you an insight into how they think that is new and helpful.

As well as noticing how they talk and the words they use, notice their pace and tone. Do they talk faster or more slowly than you? How do you feel when you match that pace – does it change how you communicate with each other?

TRY ON YOUR PARTNER'S BELIEFS

You and your partner have come to the relationship with different backgrounds, childhoods and experiences. These differences will have formed your partner into the person you fell in love with. However, as the years go by and we have children, sometimes these differences cause problems as we disagree with how to bring up the kids, the choices we make about whether to work or where to live, how to spend what disposable income we have and how to save what we can. Arguments about these important things can create fissures in the relationship that will be difficult to mend because they are caused by differences of beliefs and values.

It's much easier to change your beliefs than you might think. After all, remember that once you believed in Father Christmas or the tooth fairy and now, based on knowledge such as seeing your mum put the coin under your pillow, you don't. By being curious and through discussion, we can understand where our partner's beliefs come from and second-position ourselves to align with them. By saying to ourselves, 'If I were X and had this belief I would…' You may not agree but, by taking on the beliefs of your partner and trying them on for size, you will have a much better chance of finding a compromise that will keep you both aligned with your beliefs and values.

SECOND-POSITION YOUR FEAR

In most relationships there's an element of fear and anxiety about being left or whether your partner still loves you, feels the same or is attracted to someone else. You cannot only second-position your partner by imagining how he or she might be feeling by stepping into their shoes and seeing you from their perspective, but you can also second-position the fear itself. Fear and anxiety are there for a reason; they have a positive intention – to protect you. They may be giving you a 'heads up' or some feedback that you need to be aware of, so that you can act on it by initiating a calm discussion before things get too advanced. It probably feels a bit strange to put yourself in the position of the fear, so here's a way to do it.

Take a cushion or some object that you can say is the fear and specify what it's a fear of. Put the object on a chair and speak to it, telling it whatever you like. Then go and sit in the chair and imagine that you are that fear. What do you want to say to you (the real you)? It can be helpful to do this exercise in order to separate the fear from you because it can become so consuming that it takes over – small arguments can become massive because you've become the fear and have no control over it. It results in people distorting what's been said and adding meanings to actions that weren't intended. You have a choice in how you respond to anxiety and you will know what that choice is when you have an understanding of it by second-positioning it.

You can do this with other emotions such as anger, which is an element of fear.

Putting it all together

The ability to second-position your partner will enable you to gain a more complete understanding of your relationship, appreciate their needs and understand your own, too, in relation to them. By second-positioning, you will experience what it is like to hold their beliefs and values, and to filter their experiences in the way they do.

28

Use the three positions flexibly

CC *'It's the position from which people are assertive, expressing their view, and pursuing their own goals. If we only operated from this position we'd become egotistical, narcissistic and insensitive to the feelings of other people, and could easily end up trampling on them.'* Steve Bavister and Amanda Vickers

CC *'The ability to understand the communication loop, and the ebb and flow of events that occur within the loop, is a powerful tool, enabling people to both improve communication and produce ecological outcomes.'* Robert Dilts

CC *'The ability to move cleanly between them (the three positions), consciously or unconsciously, is necessary to act with wisdom and to appreciate the wonderful complexity of our relationships. The differences you see when you look at the world in different ways are what gives it richness and what gives you choice.'* Joseph O'Connor and John Seymour

CC *'People always tell me with absolute certainty that they don't trust themselves.'* Richard Bandler

CC *'The reason people have problems is that they have too much time to think.'* Richard Bandler

There are three ways we can perceive our world, and the ability to use all three at different times gives us the capacity to be flexible and have choices that put us in the driving seat. The three positions are first position, second position and third position. **First position** is us, our own point of view. **Second position** is the other person and **third position** is that of an impartial observer. Some call this the CCTV camera or the film director. First position is all about 'I' and 'me'. We might also refer to it as the 'associated' position.

It is important to be able to 'second-position' and put yourself into the shoes of the other person and consider their needs. However, a lot of women (not so often men) do this so much that they lose sight of themselves. When we find ourselves saying 'yes' when we mean 'no' and agreeing to do things we don't want to do so that the other person likes us, then we are moving too far towards second position.

When we disassociate and view almost any interaction from a distance without getting involved, we have become the third position, which is useful as a quick check on what is happening in the interaction but not the place to stay if you want to create good relationships and rapport.

What about the situation where we are so self-absorbed that we neglect everyone else's needs and just think about ourselves? There are certain situations where it is important to do this because otherwise how can we make decisions about our career, life choices about marriage and relationships, having a baby, moving and other life-changing decisions? Of course, there will be other people involved in these decisions but, unless you know where you stand yourself, you could end up being persuaded to do something that you might later regret.

A good place to start is by thinking about your **values**. Values are those things that you would stand up for, fight for perhaps, certainly feel strongly about. We learn values from our parents usually, either directly through what they say or indirectly, through seeing what they do and how they live their life. As children, we are constantly observing and being curious, watching how our parents do things and we then repeat their actions ourselves. Our parents are our model just as you are a model for your own children, if you have any. These values will be adhered to because they are important to us. When we do something that is not in line with our values we feel it in our body. We feel misaligned. Many physiotherapists will notice that, when they treat people for back pain, it stems from being misaligned and that our body is reflecting this and takes the emotion into itself. The physiotherapist can realign you temporarily, but to get alignment long term you need to make fundamental changes.

WHO ARE YOU?

This is an opportunity to think about your identity; who you are. Sometimes it helps to think about your purpose first. What would you like people to say about you? What would you like to be remembered for?

He/she was a great at ...

I'll always remember x for the way they ...

Some people imagine what might be written on their tombstone. It's about our legacy. Another way of thinking about it is to wonder who would play you in a film of your life. What is your mission?

Once you've decided what your mission in life is, then we can work on alignment so that every part of you is 'singing from the same hymn sheet'. If your purpose is this, then what must your values be? Do you have those values? Do you have any values that won't align and, if so, are you prepared to set them aside?

Check that your beliefs will fit with this purpose. Write a list of the sort of beliefs it would be useful to have in order to set about this purpose that you have defined and tick those you have already. Then look at the remaining beliefs. Perhaps you have them in another part of your life and can transfer them to where you need them now.

Think about the skills you need to achieve your purpose and tick those you have already. You can learn the others, so they can go on your 'to do' list.

In order to align to your purpose, you need to be doing the things that fit and prioritizing them. We often think about what we want to be doing but keep putting it off because we are committed to other things. Stop. Now is the time to first-position and concentrate on what needs to be done to achieve your purpose.

Lastly, do those around you, at home and at work, support you? How can you make changes in your environment in order to be fully aligned?

This is how absorbed you need to be if you want to achieve your purpose in life.

DO AN ECOLOGY CHECK

An NLP ecology check is what we do to ensure that no one else is going to be adversely affected by us and what we want to do. The reason we are focusing on ourselves is because we want to make a change in our life but this will affect others. Currently, you may be in a problem state and want a solution, but those around you may not be experiencing a problem state. In fact, for them, your solution may be their problem. While you are not responsible for their happiness, their resistance will not help you achieve what you want. Therefore it is essential to consider how your purpose and identity are going to impact on their lives. Ask yourself:

- What will happen if I do this?
- What will happen if I don't do this?
- What is the impact on.............if I do this?
- Is it worth it?

You may decide to delay what you want to do or slightly change it to reduce the impact on others you care about.

The ecology check is like a health check to make sure that the implications of what you want aren't detrimental when you look at the bigger picture.

MOVING BETWEEN FIRST AND SECOND POSITION

When we are in first position and thinking about our feelings and needs, we aren't considering those of the other person (second position) and that is sometimes important because, in order to align ourselves, it is our own values and beliefs that form who we are, not someone else's. However, if we were to do this all the time, people would find us unbearably selfish. We do need to be able to access the second position to check how the other person is feeling, how they respond and that what you mean to communicate is understood.

It is also essential for rapport building to be in tune with the other person and you can only be in rapport by being aware of how they process. We need to notice whether they prefer visual, auditory or kinaesthetic communication, whether they like detail or big chunk, process or choices.

When we are self-absorbed we may find ourselves communicating in a way that the other person finds offensive or confusing. People who communicate in concepts can seem vague and confusing to someone who needs detail. Equally, someone who thrives on choices can be offended when given a list of tasks or very specific instructions. A visual person who speaks quickly can find that a slower-talking auditory person takes too long to communicate and they may get distracted. Somebody who is kinaesthetic may appear fidgety and distracted by a calmer auditory person who pays a lot of attention to the words he or she uses.

In order to ensure that we are in rapport, which is the best place to be when communicating, we need to access the second position, the other person – both as an ecology check but also to know that we are communicating what and how we intend.

Putting it all together

While we need to know what we want, our purpose and our identity in order to align ourselves – which demands a time in first position – this is too self-absorbed for healthy relationships where being in rapport requires us to access second position. Underpinning all the NLP skills and techniques is the requirement to do an ecology check with ourselves to ensure that we are aligned with those with whom we live and work.

(29) Question limiting beliefs

 'Being challenged in life is inevitable, being defeated is optional.'
Roger Crawford

 'We would accomplish many more things if we did not think of them as impossible.' Chrétien Malesherbes

 'If a man harbors any sort of fear, it percolates through all his thinking, damages his personality, makes him a landlord to a ghost.' Lloyd C. Douglas

 'The outer limit of your potential is determined solely by your own beliefs and your own confidence in what you think is possible.' Brian Tracy

 'You begin to fly when you let go of self-limiting beliefs and allow your mind and aspirations to rise to greater heights.'
Brian Tracy

 'Self-pity is our worst enemy, and if we yield to it, we can never do anything wise in the world.' Helen Keller

'Yes, you can be a dreamer and a doer too, if you will remove one word from your vocabulary: impossible.' Robert Schuller

'To grow, you must be willing to let your present and future be totally unlike your past. Your history is not your destiny.'
Alan Cohen

A **belief** is something you hold to be true. Beliefs provide a framework for how we live our life, what we do and say, whom we are friends with, the work we do and so on. They are not facts, although sometimes we treat them as such and when a belief gets in the way of something we'd like to do, we call it a **limiting belief.**

A limiting belief can be that irritating and mischievous inner dialogue telling you that you 'can't' do something or an excuse for not doing something (e.g. 'it's too hard') or it can present itself as a sick feeling in the stomach when you think about doing something. It's preventing you from achieving what is possible for you. It does not allow you to experience new and exciting things such as jobs, relationships, travel opportunities and other adventures and it holds you back from your own excellence in whatever field you choose to explore.

When we have an unpleasant experience, we often distort it by generalizing – for example, 'I *never* can hit a ball straight', 'I've *always* been useless at maths', '*Everyone* knows it can't be done by that date', '*No one* can work with her.' These generalizations then become 'rules' and we don't dare to challenge them because, after all, everyone knows this, don't they?

Another way we compound a negative experience is to distort it by suggesting that it wasn't our choice to respond in the way we did. We imply that it is the fault or responsibility of others and do not own up to it being our responsibility. For example, we might say 'Flying always makes me scared' or 'They make me so angry I can't do business with them' or 'The traffic made me late.' What about 'Dieting makes you fat' as an excuse for not watching what you eat? Another type of distortion is when we extrapolate from one experience a meaning that isn't necessarily so. For example, you may have had one bad sea crossing on a ferry but this doesn't mean that you can't ever go in a boat of any kind and it doesn't mean that, should you take another sea crossing on a ferry, that the same thing would happen again. This is a 'that means that…'-type distortion.

The third way we allow limiting beliefs to take root is by deleting content, which means that we take one experience and consider it only at a vague level. Maybe we once tried to play tennis and weren't very good, so from that we say we can't do racquet sports and we're useless at tennis. However, perhaps the racquet was the wrong size or weight; maybe we were playing with a much better player or someone who wasn't playing very considerately and sending all the balls hard down the side of the court. We were young then and had never had any lessons, so what we really need to do is be specific and recognize that the belief is ill founded.

IS IT TIME TO SPRING-CLEAN YOUR BELIEF SYSTEM?

Your beliefs affect the results you'll get in life, so how about getting rid of the clutter so you can see what positive and empowering beliefs you have that you may not be able to see clearly because of all the other stuff getting in the way?

It's easy to find that those big barriers to success are masking some very useful enabling skills and some positive beliefs around your goals.

Thinking about what you currently want to achieve in a particular area of your life, make a list of all the beliefs you have around this that are not proving to be very useful.

Once you have a good long list to work with, start looking at each one individually and ask of it these questions:

1. Who says this is true?
2. Why did you believe them?
3. Do you still believe it?
4. What do they (or you) get out of believing it to be true?
5. Has it ever been true?
6. What evidence do you have for this belief?
7. What difference would it make to you if you could prove it isn't true?
8. What evidence do you need to change this belief?

As you question each belief, if it does not survive the questioning, cross it out and celebrate. You are decluttering and without that belief you'll be more resourceful and one step closer to achieving the thing you want.

Now have a look at what you're left with. These will be beliefs for which you have some evidence and ones given to you from someone you held in esteem such as a teacher or parent. What you need to do now is question each more closely.

1. Is this belief always true in every situation? Remove any generalizations such as 'always', 'never', 'everyone' and so on.
2. Is this belief a true reflection or conclusion based on one experience, or is it possible that you'd get a different response now?
3. What would you do differently if you could pretend this belief wasn't true? This is called acting 'as if'.
4. What would you rather do – keep the belief or ditch it and do something different?

You now have permission to clear all that clutter away and move forward with only your empowering beliefs.

PERCEPTUAL POSITIONING

A really good technique for questioning limiting beliefs is to use perceptual positioning. Take three chairs and place them in a triangle. One will be called first position, the second chair will be second position and the third one will be third position. First position is you, second position is the limiting belief and third position is an impartial observer or CCTV camera.

Sit at first position and talk about what you want to do, your compelling outcome. This is what is on your mind now, the thing you want to do that the limiting belief is preventing or making difficult.

When you've said what you have to say, move to second position where you speak as the limiting belief. Tell first position why you're making his/her life difficult. Really get into it – associate into the limiting belief as if you are it, not yourself.

Imagine what is in the mind of the limiting belief. What is its positive intention? What good reason does it have for limiting the ability of first position?

Now, go back to first position and respond to what second position said. Maybe you have a better understanding now of the limiting belief; maybe you can reason with it that, while they may have a good reason to protect you (this is often the motivation of a limiting belief), you may no longer need that protection and maybe it's actually holding you back now. Explain this to the limiting belief.

Now return to second position and answer this point.

You go back and forth a few times until you feel that you can move forward with the compelling outcome and no longer be limited by this belief.

Now go to third position and as an impartial observer talk about what you have noticed, what you heard from each position and what you feel is a fair conclusion and action point for the future that will satisfy first and second positions.

WRITE A POSTCARD

We're going to write a postcard to your limiting belief. This is a great way to rid yourself of limiting beliefs.

Imagine your limiting belief has gone on holiday and you are writing to it asking it never to come back again. Here's the structure:

Dear Limiting Belief,

Please stay away and don't ever come back. I am much happier without you. I am able to … and … .

Don't contact me ever again.

X

Putting it all together

Limiting beliefs have a positive intention; they are there for a reason, usually to protect us, keep us safe and stop us taking risks that we don't want to take, risks that might show us up as being vulnerable or inadequate. We simply say we 'can't' and we're off the hook. However, the opportunities that we therefore pass up could be beneficial and life-enhancing; they could mean a better job, a new relationship, different friends and new experiences. Being able to question your limiting beliefs enables you to move forward to compelling outcomes, safe in the knowledge that you have addressed their nagging worries and put them to rest where they should be – in the past and no longer relevant.

30 Conquer your fears

> ❝ *'You are born with only two fears: fear of falling and fear of loud noise. All the rest is learned. And it's a lot of work!'*
> Richard Bandler

> ❝ *'When we believe something, we act as if it is true.'* John Seymour

> ❝ *'All experience is subjective.'* Gregory Bateson

> ❝ *'It all depends how we look at things, and not on how they are themselves.'* Carl Jung

> ❝ *'Inaction breeds doubt and fear. Action breeds confidence and courage.'* Dale Carnegie

Fear is a state, not a fact. People fear different things. Some fears are unreal in that they are anxieties about what might or might not happen, such as fear of failure, while other, authentic fears, are fears of danger in the moment. Babies are not born with fear; it is learned, so it can be unlearned as well.

It is fear that protects us, stops us dawdling across a busy road in front of traffic, prevents us walking at the very edge of a cliff and makes us use oven gloves rather than picking up a pan straight from the oven. Something in our brain tells us that, if we do these things, we could be hurt – so we don't.

Fear can also raise our awareness and make us more alert for situations when we need to give our best performance as a presenter or actor. Even very accomplished presenters admit to having clammy hands and being slightly nervous before speaking, but say that this means they will give a good performance. Being relaxed doesn't bring out the best in us; we need to have that extra adrenalin that fear brings.

Many people fear dogs, injections, flying and flying insects. For the most part, these are quite normal fears and won't make life difficult because they can be overcome by 'being brave', gritting the teeth or avoiding contact with the feared thing. However, some fears cannot be avoided and, as we get older, we may have to confront them when, say, we need to take a business trip or want to travel to a developing country and need a vaccine. Fear of meeting new people has to be overcome, as we need to make friends in a new job or a new relationship, and fear of public speaking can become a problem as we move up the corporate structure or when we have to deliver a speech at a private function.

So how do we overcome these fears? In the boxes below you'll find three main methods. They are **anchoring**, which can be used for any fears and can easily be taught to your children or colleagues, the **'as if' model**, and the **fast phobia cure**, which is usually used for quite debilitating fears. The idea behind anchoring is that we create a trigger that reminds us of when we have the skill we need, be it feeling brave, calm or whatever. We practise it until every time we make that move we get that state. The fact that we can produce the state at some time means we have the skill in us as a resource. NLP thinking is that we have all the resources we need already, so even though in some situations we may experience fear, there are other situations when we don't. We are not permanently scared. Notice that people talk about 'getting into a state', but such states don't happen to us – we create them with our thinking – so by changing our thinking we can change our state. You already have unconscious anchors such as feeling hungry when you smell bacon sizzling, but here we are going to create a conscious anchor to combat your fear.

USE ANCHORING TO CONQUER YOUR FEAR

Remember Ivan Pavlov and his dogs? Every time he fed them he rang his bell so they began to develop a strong association with the bell and being fed. They even started dribbling and getting excited just on hearing it, as they knew they would soon have some food. Then he rang the bell but didn't feed them. They still salivated and got excited, even though there was no food. The bell was an anchor.

What we're going to do is create something like a bell that triggers a calm and brave state in you for managing your fear. You can't walk around with a bell in your pocket, so instead we can use an action like squeezing your earlobe, though the anchor itself is your choice. Use your anchor a few times just to check you're happy with it.

Now think about a time when you felt really brave, calm or whatever state you'd like to feel in place of the fear in the situation you dread. As you think about that great and positive feeling, give it colour and sound as if you're seeing yourself in a film of that time. Really associate into it – that means experiencing it as if it's happening right now.

When the sensation is very strong, use your anchor and, as it fades, remove it because you want to use the anchor only when the feeling is intense.

Repeat the process a few times, each time using a different example of when you experienced the state you want to anchor. In between each anchoring, just give yourself a little shake – because you need to recreate the tension of anchoring anew each time and separate each one. You may surprise yourself at how often you do experience that state, so anchor the best examples.

Now you have an anchor to use whenever you feel the fear starting to create an unresourceful state for you. Replace it with a more resourceful state using your anchor.

USE THE 'AS IF' MODEL TO CONQUER YOUR FEAR

Here you are creating a new strategy or behaviour based on how you'd like to respond to the fear trigger. It's a bit like acting or doing a dress rehearsal. We use the same thinking to create what happens as what we would like to happen.

Think of a behaviour, a reaction to a situation, that you would like to have in place of what usually happens, and imagine the desired outcome. You may want to think about someone who does that thing with excellence or a time when you didn't have the fear but had a more resourceful attitude or response. After all, we aren't born with these fears; they develop over time.

See yourself doing the new behaviour but from a distance, as if you're watching yourself do it, like a fly on the wall or a CCTV camera. You can adjust the scene however you like. You may want to change the colour, sound or size of the thing that triggers the response or change something about yourself. You can also change the other people in the scene to make it more acceptable or change their expressions, perhaps, or what they are doing.

Once you're totally happy with the changed situation and behaviour, you can step into it and adopt that behaviour for yourself, noticing the new physiology and the new responses. See, hear and feel the new experience. Practise the new behaviour as often as possible, until it becomes incorporated into your identity.

It's useful to conduct an ecology check, too, to make sure that the new behaviour aligns with your values and beliefs. If there are any problems, go back to your scene and make the necessary adjustments.

USE THE FAST PHOBIA CURE TO ELIMINATE FEAR

1. Imagine you are in a cinema sitting towards the back and you're waiting for the film to start.
2. Look up at the screen and see a black-and-white still of you, taken before the thing that you fear happened, so you look calm and relaxed.
3. Now imagine going to the projection room from where you can see yourself in the seat looking at the picture of you on the screen. You notice that both images are relaxed and calm and, indeed, that's how you feel at the moment as well.

4. Imagine that you now turn on the imaginary film from the projection room. It is in black and white and the film is of a recent phobic incident. Stop the film when it gets to the end and you can see the last shot of you as a still photo on the screen.
5. Now you're going to take yourself to the screen and put yourself where the still photo is and, as you do that, you are in full colour,
6. Now run that film backwards in colour FAST and repeat this several times.
7. You can do a quick check now and imagine the next time you encounter the phobic situation. Do you feel differently about it now?

Putting it all together

Fear is there to protect us, but there are times when fear protects us unnecessarily by holding us back from behaviour that will enhance our life, even though initially it may seem a bit scary. Using NLP techniques such as anchoring, the 'as if' strategy and the fast phobia cure remind us that before and after any frightening event we are fine and relaxed. All we need is a strategy for the bit in between. We can control our state through changing the way we think, so that we get a different, more resourceful response to events. We can't control events but we can control our response to them.

31 Get rapport quickly

> 'When we can laugh at ourselves, our issues and our worlds, then we can really be free.' Richard Bandler

> 'When you match the representational system someone is using, it makes that person feel in rapport with you. When you 'mismatch' it, they don't feel as good because they're not hearing what resonates with them.' Richard Bandler

> 'People buy people first, before they buy the product or service. However good you are at the technical aspects of selling – describing features (what the customer buys), advantages (what the features do) and benefits (what the buyer gains) – you have to be able to build rapport and win their trust first.' Steve Bavister and Amanda Vickers

> 'When you're in rapport with another person, you have the opportunity to enter her world, see things from her perspective, appreciate why she feels the way she does and arrive at a better understanding of who she is.' Roger Ellerton

> 'If you do not believe in the importance of rapport, then you may as well shut up shop now. Autocracies are dead. Hierarchies are crumbling.' Sue Knight

Rapport is the word we use to describe that feeling of connection with someone where you are conversing happily, agreeing with each other and finding lots in common. It is what most people would say is the ideal situation between two people and what we should be aiming for in most contexts – from brief interactions such as buying something from a corner shop to making a sales pitch at work. The faster we can get rapport, the sooner we can start on the content, the thing we want to communicate.

What Richard Bandler and John Grinder noticed, as they conducted their research into what differentiated those people who were successful and those who weren't, was that successful people established rapport quickly. They did this by matching each other's communication patterns on all levels – verbal and non-verbal. They found that by deliberately matching the other person's communication patterns you could create a sense of profound connection with them. This isn't about mimicking. Indeed, if you mirrored the other person's every move, you certainly wouldn't establish rapport. Rather, you notice what they do and how they do it, gradually adapting so that you are more similar to them in terms of tone of voice, tempo, pitch, speed, body movements and so on. In fact, matching the other person's breathing can be a powerful way of connecting with them.

We generally have a preference as to whether we communicate in images, sounds or action, and feelings. These are visual, auditory and kinaesthetic. When we match the same kinds of words the other person feels, we are 'speaking their language'. If you hear words like 'look' and 'see' and words that appear to be trying to conjure up images, then use the same words yourself and reassure the other person that you can 'see what they mean'. An auditory person will speak more slowly and be very careful with their choice of words, so do the same and tell them that you 'hear what they are saying'. A kinaesthetic person may well move about a bit, touch you and gesticulate, trying to communicate in body language as well as words. Lots of nodding and the reassurance that 'you get what they mean' will go down well.

When you speak to a large audience or a class, you have to use all three representational systems – visual, auditory and kinaesthetic – so that you connect with everyone. It also gives everyone a full sensory experience.

This is also true for communications you give publicly on social media, your website, forums and so on. Remember to address all representational systems so you connect with the maximum number of people. Make what you have to say punchy, correct and well expressed, addressing what will be of interest to them.

Lastly, laugh. It's the quickest way to gain rapport, as people want to know what's funny and share it with you.

PERCEPTUAL POSITIONS

Another way to get rapport quickly with someone is to enter their map of the territory. We all have different 'maps' which represent our history, beliefs and values, experiences and so on. Our territory will differ too; one person's environment is not the same as another's, so if the person you want rapport with comes from a different culture or works in a different type of organization, is a different age or has characteristics with which you aren't familiar, you will need quickly to be able to absorb their map and the information on it.

We do this by briefly leaving our body and going to what in NLP we call the 'second position'. First position is us. Second position is the other person with whom we want rapport. Third position is that of an impartial observer or witness.

Imagine what it's like to be the other person by taking the second position and be curious about what life's like for you in that mental space. You will very quickly realize what you need to do and say in order to get rapport quickly.

Go back to first position and get that rapport. If you want to check you've got it right, mentally jump to third position and observe the rapport in action. Lastly, laugh.

WANTING AND NOT WANTING

As well as the visual, auditory and kinaesthetic patterns, people also have a preference as to whether they like to think about what they want or what they don't want.

If you're selling to someone who doesn't want poor quality, doesn't want to have a huge wait for delivery and doesn't want the costly option, then match their words. It would be very tempting to assure them of your high-quality product, your great delivery schedule and your reasonable price, but this isn't in rapport. Use their words for a good and successful sales deal.

By matching how they represent information, you will get rapport quickly. As a salesperson, this may seem quite an odd sales approach, but some people live in this territory of avoiding what they don't want and tend to be risk averse. The map is not the territory. Be curious. In what way or in what part of your life do you also aim to avoid things? Maybe you eat healthy food to avoid becoming overweight; take cold remedies to avoid your cold getting worse; lecture the kids on Internet safety to keep them from making inadvisable connections online.

By being curious about what you have in common and where your similarities lie, you will succeed in gaining rapport quickly with whomever you're talking to.

FIRST IMPRESSIONS

People make decisions about whether they're going to like you before you've even spoken. They eye you up, check out what you're wearing and how you look, and then they'll decide whether or not they want to talk with you. In a business context, they or you may not have the choice – in which case, it will be harder to gain rapport if you give off the wrong signals.

Body language is hugely important. Before you even start talking, smile and be approachable. Eye contact is crucial, as is direct body connection (where you face them with your whole body). Keep your body still. Fidgeting with papers or your hair, clothes and hands can be distracting and prevents good eye contact, as the other person tries to work out what you're doing.

It has become common nowadays for people to check their cellphones while in someone else's company. This has never been nor never will be conducive to good rapport. What you're basically saying is that someone or something else is more important than they are.

Clothes say a lot about you and what's important to you, so they need to be clean and well fitting. They should also suit you and the environment you're in and whom you're with. Check the mirror before you leave the house and ask yourself, 'If I was meeting me today for the first time, what sort of person do I think I'd be?' and if that isn't who you want to be, then go and change!

On a hygiene note: smell is very powerful and people can be put off by your body odour, regardless of what you say, so make sure you smell good.

Putting it all together

Gaining rapport quickly has so many advantages in all areas of life because we live life so quickly and make connections all the time via social media, networking events, parties and online via forums and chat rooms. The overriding rule is to consciously present yourself as you want to be seen, match the other person's way of standing, talking and viewing the world and be curious. Remember: the map is not the territory.

32 Get rapport with a visual person

As we think about the world around us, we do so using images, sounds and feelings, tastes and smells – our five senses. We can't take in everything and each of us tends to notice different things. Someone whom we describe as **visual** tends to notice what they see. Someone **auditory** notices what they hear and a **kinaesthetic** person notices their feelings or actions. We use all five senses, of course, so, even when we have a preference for one, we don't not use the others. It is just a preference. Rapport is a sense of shared understanding, a sense of trust and confidence in another person. We tend to be drawn and connect most easily to those who are similar to us. If we are predominantly visual, it will seem second nature to connect with other visual people, but what if we are not? How then could we gain rapport with a visual person quickly?

In order to establish rapport, we essentially need to match the people we are communicating with. This means that, whether or not we are a visual type of person ourselves, we need to act as if we are so that the other person recognizes that we are speaking their language. We can practise this and we do this by exercising our visual skills. Start in the present and really notice what's around you right now – the colours, shapes and textures, the comparative size of things. Imagine you have to describe them to someone – how would you do that? Now visualize something that isn't here right now such as your home or workplace (depending on where you are right now). Imagine a friend of yours or a relative you know well and get a picture of them in your mind. Imagine that a burglary has taken place at work – how would you describe what is where in your office or workplace? What can you see from your bedroom window? Could you paint it in your mind?

We can take this exercise on further by imagining what we would look like with pink hair or spectacles, or both! What would you look like if you were twice the height or half the weight? Would you look good in yellow? Picture it! By flexing our visual muscles we can improve them and get a good idea of what it would be like to have a visual preference and therefore connect better with the visual people we meet.

People often choose careers that match their representational system (visual, auditory or kinaesthetic). For example, you'll find visual people in careers such as art and design, photography, graphics and so on. If you regularly work with people in these fields, it will enhance your communications with them when you match them.

A visual person will look for people to connect with who also look like visual people, although they won't necessarily be aware that they are doing it. They are instinctively drawn to other visuals, possibly because they see that they also take care with their appearance and they will already have been spotted by them. Visuals are always looking around them, taking in their environment, noticing all the visual cues. They will easily be upset by mess or colours they don't like. They themselves will be aware of how they look and how they fit into the space. Their appearance is important, so you need to appreciate it too, although, depending on the situation and your relationship, it may not be appropriate to mention it.

MIRRORING

When you want to achieve rapport with a visual person, you need to match their body language – first, because that is the greatest part of establishing rapport. This is done by mirroring and there are four key techniques, explained below:

1. **Match voice tone or tempo or both:** Notice whether tones are high or low, loud or soft. Is the tempo fast or slow? Are there pauses or no pauses? This is, of course, particularly relevant for phone calls, Skype and conference calls where there is little or no visual connection. When you match tone and tempo, do it gradually so it doesn't sound false.
2. **Match breathing:** Watch for the breathing rhythm by observing movement in the shoulders and chest, then pace it.
3. **Match movement:** It would be very obvious if you copied exactly what the other person does, so, instead, when they make a movement, you should do a similar but not identical one– for example, if they tap your foot, you could tap your pen.
4. **Match body posture:** Mirror their body posture, so lean forward when they do and lean back when they lean back. Avoid exact mimicry and delay your movement so that it doesn't look obvious. What you're aiming for is a natural mirroring such as you get when two people know each other very well.

WORDS USED BY A VISUAL PERSON

Visual people will talk about 'seeing the light at the end of the tunnel', 'seeing their way to a solution', 'not seeing the wood for the trees', 'watching out for something', 'looking for a way forward' and ask for your 'view' on something.

Here's a list of words and phrases that mark someone out as visual. By using these expressions yourself you will connect easily with them:

- appear
- bird's-eye view
- catch a glimpse of
- clarify
- clear-cut
- dark
- dress up
- enlighten
- examine
- expose
- focus
- glance
- glimpse
- graphic
- hazy idea
- hindsight
- illusion
- in the light of
- in view of
- look
- look into
- make a scene
- mind's eye
- notice
- obvious
- outlook
- perspective
- pinpoint
- reveal
- see
- short-sighted
- spectacle
- take a dim view of
- tunnel vision
- under your nose
- vague

(from *Essential NLP* by Steve Bavister and Amanda Vickers)

HOW TO RECOGNIZE A VISUAL PERSON

Visual people will tend to have their head up and they'll be clearly visually aware, looking around the room, perhaps, looking out for someone they know or looking directly about two foot in front of them. They probably won't look at the person they're talking to because this interferes with them accessing their images. They tend to look up and to the left when they're recalling something they've seen before and up and to the right if they're trying to imagine something.

They may well be using gestures, pointing things out to someone. There will be some tension in the body, as they tend to be alert and body conscious because this tightening tends to make their pictures clearer.

You will hear that their voice is fairly high pitched and they tend to talk quite fast as they retrieve images from their head and relay them to the listener. Their breathing therefore tends to be quite shallow.

When people don't know about the different representational systems, they're inclined to expect everyone to be like them. Visual people wonder why others don't notice their frustration with an untidy room or their concern that their clothes don't look good, but for auditory people they're focusing on what you're saying and a kinaesthetic person is watching what you're doing. Our focus is different depending on how we process our world, and this makes our map different from someone else's map. We can achieve the best rapport by stepping into the other person's map and communicating within it.

33 Get rapport with an auditory person

66 *'When our audience reads or watches our work, their internal representational systems create or recreate the sights, sounds, actions, feelings, tastes and smells. As their representational systems are stimulated, they become engaged with our work.'* Bekki Hill

66 *'When two people share the same preferred representational system, conversations and interactions run very smoothly. You can both see very clearly where you are aiming to get to, you hear the same details of the interaction and you both feel the same way about the purpose of your shared dialogue.'* Jeff Archer

66 *'Listening is the highest form of courtesy.'* Tom Peters

66 *'It is better to remain silent at the risk of being thought a fool than to talk and remove all doubt of it.'* Maurice Switzer

66 *'Two monologues do not make a dialogue.'* Jeff Daly

Rapport is the word we use to describe the very easy comfortable feeling you have when you and another person are communicating well. Sometimes, you notice the absence of it more than its presence, especially if you usually find it quite easy to connect with people and 'get on with them'. There are usually some people we get on with better than others and these are probably people who view the world similarly to you.

As we have seen, there are three main views on the world: visual, auditory and kinaesthetic. **Visual** is when you notice what you see predominantly; **auditory** is what we call people who notice what is said and what they hear, and **kinaesthetic** people prefer action and feelings to words and pictures. In order to improve rapport, it works best to match the representational system of the person you're talking to.

When we want to connect better with an auditory person, we can prepare and increase our auditory skills by becoming more aware of the sounds around us. Stop what you are doing and just be still. Listen. There's rarely silence. There will be sounds, even if it's just the hum of domestic appliances, computer fans and so on. Even people working quietly make sounds as they type, write notes, fiddle with things and maybe sigh. So concentrate on the present and what you can hear now. Then think about and recall the sounds you usually hear but can't hear now, like the sound of your car, your child, your dog or cat, the theme tune of your favourite soap. Can you conjure up nails going down a blackboard, tyres screeching, a baby screaming, a car alarm? What about your favourite piece of music, a song from your favourite band? Test yourself – can you hum or sing the national anthem or another well-known song? What would a barking budgie sound like or a humming hippo… a crying car? How about making up a tune right now?

Rapport is important between teacher and pupil, manager and trainee, parent and child, because we all learn differently. A visual learner will want to read a written text or read the lesson from the board, but an auditory learner will prefer to listen to the lesson and have the opportunity to ask questions. Kinaesthetic learners want to have a go themselves; they like interactive lessons. If you're working with an auditory learner, make sure you talk slowly so that they can process what you say. Let them read out parts of the text and ask questions. They will work well in groups and find it hard to remain quiet. They tend to be good at spoken subjects such as languages and they'll have good pronunciation. They are usually good at music but they may not necessarily be musical. When helping an auditory learner, suggest that they record the lesson and use the Internet to watch videos to support the material you provide.

HOW TO RECOGNIZE AN AUDITORY PERSON

You may well hear an auditory person before you see them! Their speech is quite slow and purposeful, as they think carefully about each word they choose. Their tone is clear and precise, and they pace their speech more slowly than a visual person, though not as slowly as a kinaesthetic. They may think aloud, working through a situation or repeating what's been said so they get clarity. They may just want a sounding board rather than genuinely being interested in your opinion.

Breathing is across the chest, and they may well stand quite still, possibly with their arms folded.

An auditory person tends to tilt their head to one side as if listening.

WORDS USED BY AN AUDITORY PERSON

Here's a list of words and phrases that mark someone out as auditory. By using these expressions yourself you will connect easily with them.

- audible
- call
- clear as a bell
- clearly expressed
- compose
- discuss
- earful
- earshot
- harmonize
- hear
- hidden message
- listen
- loud and clear
- manner of speaking
- mention
- note
- outspoken
- remark
- report
- say
- scream
- shout
- silence
- sing
- sound
- speechless
- tell the truth
- tongue-tied
- tune-in
- voice
- well-informed
- word for word

(from *Essential NLP* by Steve Bavister and Amanda Vickers)

TRY WHOLE-BODY LISTENING

When our attention is internal, we are inclined to make judgements and evaluations as we hear what the other person is saying and compare it with what we think, our values and beliefs. We are actually distracted from what they are saying as we consider what we have to say on the subject. This internal focus means that we are inward-looking, quite possibly also in the literal sense because we may not even be looking at the person who is talking. Perhaps we're looking down, reflecting on what we think, looking at another person to see whether they agree with you or looking elsewhere as we signal our disagreement and think of a good response. Evidence of this can be heard in statements beginning 'I', where beliefs are expressed as facts.

Instead, try whole-body listening. Pay attention to what the other person is saying and be curious about their map of the world. Look at them and mirror their body posture and movements, though not in an obvious way, of course.

Most importantly, match their language pattern, so use visual words and phrases for someone who is using them; auditory words for someone who prefers to focus on what they hear; and kinaesthetic words for people who prefer action and feelings.

Putting it all together

Auditory people love conversations and they will seek you out for one if they can – they will prefer that to emails or texts. If you do business with someone you've identified as auditory, make sure that you phone them and be prepared for a long chat! Match their pace and tone, volume and the words they use, sentence length and other sounds they make such as 'ums' and 'ahs', chuckles and silences. All these form their preferred pattern. They will appreciate it and your communication will have great rapport. People do business with people they like and people who they feel are like them.

(34) Get rapport with a kinaesthetic person

CC *'Rapport has become a vital skill on which to pin the success of your business. Through your ability to build rapport you can help other people feel at ease in your company – they choose to be with you because you make it easy for them to be so. People relate to you and the services you offer because they feel you are sympathetic to their needs.'* Sue Knight

CC *'Kinos wiggle a lot.'* Genie Z. Laborde

CC *'One skill shared by outstanding performers in any field is to be able to move easily through all the representational systems and use the most appropriate one for the task in hand.'* Joseph O'Connor

CC *'For kinaesthetic people planning the future is like trying on a new outfit. It can take a little bit of time to future plan all sensations and emotions, so processing feelings can be slower than processing pictures or sounds, but only by exploring the full range of positive feelings that will result from making progress will you be able to plan the right approach for you and then follow it through.'* Jeff Archer

CC *'In a relationship with a kinesthetic oriented person, if you don't touch them often, they may not feel loved by you. They may feel rejected and not even know why. If your loved one is saying things like, "You never touch me," or "You never cuddle with me anymore," their love tank may be empty. Fill it up with some meaningful and long snuggles on the couch, a big* *bear hug or a nice back massage. Then keep their hearts filled by giving them the touching, hugging, and snuggling they are thirsting for.'* Wil Dieck

Having rapport with someone is about feeling comfortable around them, trusting them and them returning your trust. It works best when you have a philosophy of rapport in everyday life rather than turning it on like a tap when you need to make a sale or convince someone to adopt your strategy. A kinaesthetic person will be quite active and physical. Feelings will matter a lot and they'll be aware of the atmosphere between you. Words will be less important to a kinaesthetic person; they will be more likely to connect and establish rapport if they feel comfortable around you.

People with a kinaesthetic preference aren't too bothered about what things look or sound like; they want to get to grips with it, touch it, feel it, do it themselves. They need longer to consider a situation and work out how they feel about it, but they don't like long periods of inactivity. If you do business with a kinaesthetic person, keep them involved in what's happening, give them something to do and ensure that there are breaks during long meetings so they can get up and move about. If appropriate, give them product to feel and play with and paper to write on. Keep the speed of presenting down and ask questions so that they feel involved and that what they think is important. Give them a job to do such as taking minutes, recording on a flip chart or passing round notes. They will prefer one-to-one chats rather than emails, texts or phone calls.

Studies have shown that only 7 per cent of what is communicated between people is transmitted through words themselves and 38 per cent comes through tone of voice, leaving 55 per cent communicated by physiology or body language. This is particularly relevant for connecting with kinaesthetic people, for whom touch and physical contact are important. They can easily feel overwhelmed in verbal conflict and can let their emotions rule their heads. They tend to make decisions based on gut feeling rather than logic.

To get in touch with your kinaesthetic side, remember what it's like having your feet tickled, running with the wind in your hair, making a snowman, jumping over stepping stones or riding a bike. Imagine that you are swimming – how does the water feel as you push it away with your hands, and how does it feel kicking with your feet? How does it feel being weightless in the water? Remember being young, having lots of energy and being physical. Think about what being cold is like and being hot – how warm do you feel at the moment? Become aware of your body now and notice which parts are tense and which are relaxed, which parts are touching the surface of your chair and where you can feel clothes touching your skin. Now think about how you're feeling and what's important to you.

PACING AND LEADING

In order to build rapport, we match the other person's body language, verbal language and their behaviour. We 'pace' it. By doing this, we step into the other person's shoes and experience life as them for a few moments. It's rather like walking beside them at the same pace and being in their map of the world.

As you build rapport such that you feel connected and in tune with them, you feel at one with them. They also feel the connection and it becomes difficult to tell who is pacing whom. However, you may be the teacher or employer and want them to tackle a difficult issue that they're avoiding or you need them to be in a more resourceful state. Perhaps you're in a selling situation and need to turn the topic of conversation towards the product you're selling. You can gradually take over the lead if you are in a situation where you want to bring them round to a different way of thinking. You can't lead them until this rapport is established.

Once you are successfully matching them and they are matching you, change one thing slightly to test whether they will start to match you. This could just be pace of speech, pitch or tone. It could be choice of words or body language. Very subtly, you should be able to take over the lead and take the conversation where you want to go. Rapport doesn't have to be about agreement; you can disagree in rapport.

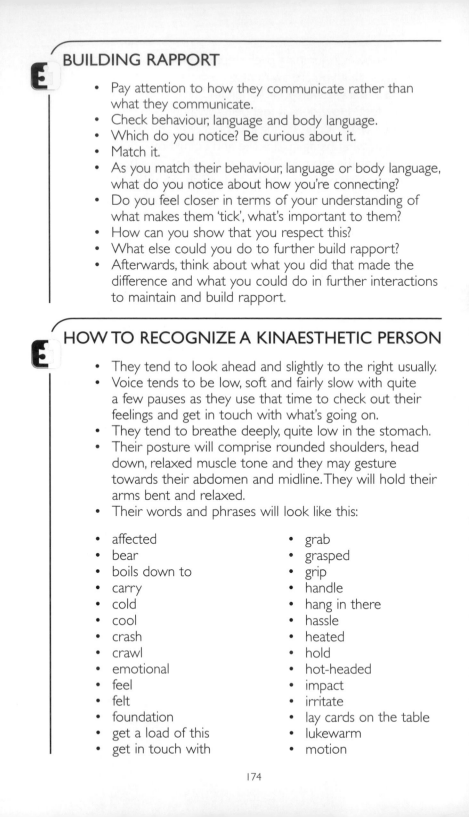

BUILDING RAPPORT

- Pay attention to how they communicate rather than what they communicate.
- Check behaviour, language and body language.
- Which do you notice? Be curious about it.
- Match it.
- As you match their behaviour, language or body language, what do you notice about how you're connecting?
- Do you feel closer in terms of your understanding of what makes them 'tick', what's important to them?
- How can you show that you respect this?
- What else could you do to further build rapport?
- Afterwards, think about what you did that made the difference and what you could do in further interactions to maintain and build rapport.

HOW TO RECOGNIZE A KINAESTHETIC PERSON

- They tend to look ahead and slightly to the right usually.
- Voice tends to be low, soft and fairly slow with quite a few pauses as they use that time to check out their feelings and get in touch with what's going on.
- They tend to breathe deeply, quite low in the stomach.
- Their posture will comprise rounded shoulders, head down, relaxed muscle tone and they may gesture towards their abdomen and midline. They will hold their arms bent and relaxed.
- Their words and phrases will look like this:

- affected
- bear
- boils down to
- carry
- cold
- cool
- crash
- crawl
- emotional
- feel
- felt
- foundation
- get a load of this
- get in touch with

- grab
- grasped
- grip
- handle
- hang in there
- hassle
- heated
- hold
- hot-headed
- impact
- irritate
- lay cards on the table
- lukewarm
- motion

- muddled
- nail
- pressure
- rub
- shallow
- sharpen
- shift
- shock
- slipped my mind
- solid
- sore
- stir
- stress
- strike
- tap
- throw
- tickle
- tied up
- touch
- weighed heavily
- wring

(From *Essential NLP* by Steve Bavister and Amanda Vickers)

Putting it all together

To get rapport with a kinaesthetic person, pay particular attention to body language and meet them face to face rather than trying to connect via email or the phone. Plan an activity together and give them an active role. Know that, for them, it needs to 'feel right' rather than trying to persuade them with words and figures. Match their kinaesthetic words and phrases, allowing pauses for them to check in with their sense of whether it feels right to them.

35 Teach effectively with VAK

> ❝ 'Rather than tailoring teaching techniques to each individual, a combination of simultaneous congruent stimuli will enable an entire classroom to improve their encoding, storing and retrieval of information.' Nick Grist

> ❝ 'Develop your senses... realize that everything connects to everything else.' Leonardo da Vinci

> ❝ 'Who dares to teach must never cease to learn.' John Cotton Dana

> ❝ 'Whoever has the ability to adapt to the other person's way of thinking will get better results.' Joseph O'Connor

> ❝ 'It is important to have a wide range of different learning strategies in order to be successful in a variety of different types of tasks. NLP believes it is better to develop flexibility to learn through several different strategies, rather than rigidly using one.' Tad James

Children learn in different ways, at different speeds and focus on different aspects of what they are taught so teachers need to present their material in several different ways to ensure that all of the class glean the key information. Visual learners need to see things, auditory learners need to hear and kinaesthetic learners need to experience. Teaching needs to cover all these. Research in this area has shown that, when teachers use a multisensory approach, children learn better as opposed to tailoring the approach on an individual child basis.

There are a number of theories of how people learn and one of them is that we learn using a preferred sensory style – visual, auditory or kinaesthetic. **Visual** refers to what we see, **auditory** is what we hear and kinaesthetic is what we do or feel. We have access to all these and use different ones for different parts of our life, but when it comes to most things we have a preferred style. Teachers need to cover all three as they teach a class, but when you need to communicate with a child who is struggling, you can make a breakthrough by using their preferred style. If you think of what yours is and then remember which teachers and which subjects you enjoyed most at school, you may find a link between your preferred style and the subject and teacher's teaching style. If you are a teacher, what is your preferred style? Think about how you could adapt how you teach to more successfully communicate with learners who prefer different styles. Interestingly, we are taught differently as we move up the key stages at school; starting by learning by doing and experimenting (kinaesthetically), then through whiteboard ('talk and chalk') and hand-outs (visually), then at university through lectures (auditory).

Simply the process of thinking about how we learn and how we teach increases awareness and this in turn increases flexibility. By recognizing our preferred patterns, we can swiftly adapt the style being used to suit us by asking for a verbal explanation (auditory) or to have something written down (visual) or to go through it again (kinaesthetic). In life, though, one cannot exist by only being taught one way or only being able to process in one way. Awareness enables us to ensure that all three learning and teaching styles are embraced for a truly multisensory experience.

While awareness of learning styles in schools and among teachers is high, even to the extent that in some schools students wear badges with 'V', 'A' or 'K' on them, in the workplace it is almost unknown despite it being a very active learning and teaching environment. In large companies with induction schemes for new employees, the materials are rarely presented in a multisensory fashion. Similarly, information about health and safety and working practices will be presented as written documents. When you need to explain something to a colleague, do you consider whether to use their preferred style or do you simply use your own and expect them to understand? Next time, work out what 'language' they speak and use the same. That way, you will create good rapport and quickly communicate the information to them. If someone is passing on information to you, be aware of which representational system they are using, and if it doesn't match yours, you could ask them to explain it (auditory), show you (visual) or walk you through it (kinaesthetic).

In the sports world, if you are training someone, find out their preferred learning style. Telling someone how to perform a powerful serve will work for an auditory person, showing them for a visual person, while a kinaesthetic person will want to have a go themselves and practise until it feels right to them.

TEACHING VISUAL LEARNERS

- Visual learners need pictures and drawings. So, for them, visual aids are important – slides, diagrams, charts and hand-outs. They need to see words written. Ask them to write down as you speak, taking notes and organizing them so they can see different sections and subsections easily.
- Encourage them to use mind maps, flow diagrams, charts and pictures to aid understanding of the subject.
- Find other presentation styles than simply telling facts, such as using videos, so that they have visual representation. Find pictures and photographs and maps to stimulate their learning and engagement.
- Leave plenty of white space on hand-outs so they make notes; flip charts will also help, as will other visual aids such as whiteboards and images pinned around the room.
- Use words like 'see', 'look', 'view', 'draw', 'picture', 'imagine', 'focus'.
- You can recognize visual learners from their eye movements. They tend to look around a lot, look upward, accessing visual memories (looking up and left), or trying to work out a visual solution (up and right). Their breathing tends to be shallow and fast, matching their higher-pitched and faster speech as they try to communicate verbally from the images in their head.

TEACHING AUDITORY LEARNERS

- Auditory learners listen and notice rhythms and sound patterns. They appreciate discussions, tapes and recordings. They learn by repeating words. They may even appear to be repeating words to themselves as they write in the classroom and they would prefer to tell you their answer rather than write it down. They will want to read out loud rather than read to themselves, and you will probably see their mouth moving as they read.
- When teaching in this style, introduce the lesson by telling them what you're going to be covering in the lesson and finishing with a summary of what's been covered.
- During the lesson, ask questions and encourage conversation, possibly using mini-groups reporting back what they've discovered or discussed.
- Get students to read out sections of the text they are reading or their answers to questions that they've written down.
- Use words like: 'hear', 'listen', 'speak', 'talk', 'sounds', 'tell me', 'say'.
- Auditory learners are the chatty ones! They talk more slowly, though, than visual learners, so, when talking to them, match their tone and pace, which will be both lower and slower. They breathe more deeply and will tend to look down as they think about what they want to say and find the right words to express it.

TEACHING KINAESTHETIC LEARNERS

- Kinaesthetic learners notice gestures and body movements. They learn by actively doing and participating. They learn best through the experience of science experiments, role play, projects and active exploration. It is important for them to have regular breaks to allow movement, otherwise they will get fidgety and easily distracted.
- Get them doing things such as taking notes, underlining key points, colouring in, finding facts in the text, listening out for details on something.
- Active learning is key for them, so get them up and moving, give them jobs to do like handing out materials, tidying away, sorting things out, writing on the flip chart.

- They will want to engage on different levels, so get them writing things up on the board, copying down material on their hand-out, typing in on the computer and discussing in groups.
- They'll enjoy field trips and school outings to visit places of interest – castles, museums (with interactive exhibits) and geological/geographic features.
- Words you can use to engage with kinaesthetic learners are: 'do', 'make', 'find', 'discover', 'get', 'walk', 'run', 'grab', 'take', 'feel'.
- Kinaesthetic learners will be fidgety and active. They do things rather than talk about them, and are impatient for the lesson to be over so they can go outside and run about.

Putting it all together

While we tend to have a preferred learning style and teaching style, we need to be aware of what it is and adapt it when communicating information to someone with a different preference. Ideally, using a multisensory approach, we engage with everyone.

(36) Learn visually

CC *'To be able to visualize in rich detail, to be able to hold an image so steady you can copy from it, to be able to instantly access large amounts of information, is a skill so significantly valuable for succeeding in school.'* Don Blackerby

'When we understand the nature of our representations, we begin to influence our thinking, our emotions and consequently our experience. What we think is what we are.' Sue Knight

CC *'People vary a great deal in how easily and vividly they can visualize but everyone can improve their clarity and control by practising. Everyone has a photographic memory but some people have better quality film in their camera.'* Joseph O'Connor

CC *'A lot of schoolchildren have problems learning simply because of a mismatch between the primary representational system of the teacher and that of the child. If neither one of them has the flexibility to adjust, no learning occurs.'* Richard Bandler and John Grinder

'Life is not the way it's supposed to be, it's the way it is. The way you cope with it is what makes the difference.' Virginia Satir

Knowing how you learn, how you process information generally and how you communicate means that you will be able to select the optimum teaching and communication environment. You will understand why you get on better with some communicators than with others and why you are better with some content than others. In an ideal world, though, we need to communicate in every way – visually, auditorially and kinaesthetically – but the skill of being able to adapt what we are given to suit our learning style means that we can always improve our experience.

Sixty-five per cent of the population are visual learners, with visual learning defined as 'keeping pictures in our heads'. This is the first skill babies are tested for at six weeks when they are checked to find out whether they recognize their mother. They do, of course, but if Mum then puts on a pink curly wig they will cry because the picture doesn't match the picture they have in their head. When people learn visually, they make pictures in their head and it is easiest when teaching visual learners to teach them through the pictures they generate. Indeed, 90 per cent of the information that comes into our brain is visual. Visual learners notice what they see and are very observant. They can easily switch from a 2D image and imagine the 3D version, so, for example, they can see a picture of a house and then imagine it in 3D. While this is an essential skill for architects and designers, it can be quite confusing when children are learning to read and the 2D images of the letters become 3D and move about.

When children learn visually, they see a picture of the word and associate it with the picture of the meaning of the word, and so, if they are counting, they visualize, say, two apples and three apples. In order to access their visual memory, they need to look up, so do this if you're a visual learner, and if you are a teacher, be sure to tell children who learn visually to look up. Some teachers have been known to tell children gazing up into space, 'You won't find the answer up there,' but actually they will!

Words to use when teaching or communicating with a visual learner include: 'see', 'look', 'view', 'appear', 'show', 'reveal', 'imagine', 'clear', 'focused', 'hazy', 'picture'. When they 'don't see what you mean' you will need to 'show them again'.

Use diagrams, maps, mind maps, graphs, colours and pictures to teach visual learners and, if you are the student, take what you are told and represent it visually to make it easier to learn. You probably already love drawing and doodling with colours, so you'll not need any prompting. You enjoy organizing your notes into coloured folders or with file tabs and different-coloured dividers.

Careers that will suit you will be artistic ones such as photography, video or film, design, planning, art, architecture and similar.

HOW DO YOU KNOW IF YOU'RE VISUAL?

Of course, you won't only be visual; you will have times when you are enjoying your auditory and kinaesthetic processing systems, but you can check which your preferred one is quite easily by doing the following:

- Thinking about yesterday, what comes to mind? Are you thinking about what you saw, what you heard or what you did?
- When you think about your holiday plans, do you imagine where you'd like to go, remember what people have told you about somewhere, or think about what you'd like to do on holiday?
- In conversation with friends, do you notice how they're dressed and their facial expressions, do you pay attention to what they're saying, or do you notice what they're doing?
- Picture an elephant. Is it still or moving? Where is it? If you're a visual learner you will have lots of information about that elephant going on in your head at the same time. You'll also have a choice and can picture it in different locations, in different sizes and doing different things quite easily, because for a visual learner the image will probably be moving and changing all the time.
- Just as visual people pay attention to what they see and like to have nice things around them, they will be upset by untidiness or ugly buildings, unattractive people or unpleasant areas. If you find yourself feeling like that, then you are probably visual.

HOW CAN YOU TELL IF SOMEONE IS VISUAL BEFORE YOU'VE SPOKEN TO THEM?

There are often occasions when you want to be in rapport with someone but don't know yet which representational system they prefer. It could be at a party or a meeting, perhaps. They will be communicating, of course, from the moment you see them, so check out their body language. Visual people often sit bolt upright and their eyes are darting everywhere. They give good eye contact and flick their eyes upwards frequently as they search for the images in their head – up left for 'visual remembered' and up and to the right for 'visual constructed'. They will be focusing intently on what is being shown or on what they are reading, and will not be distracted by the noise of someone entering the room, coughing or making an aside to their neighbour at the meeting.

NLP SPELLING STRATEGY

- Take a word you find difficult to spell and one you want to be able to spell correctly.
- Write it on a piece of paper. If it's a long word, break it up into smaller chunks by syllables or parts if it's a compound word. Use different colours for the different parts of the word and write it large, bold and clear.
- Now take each part in turn and look at it while you recite the letters forming each chunk.
- Practise by removing it from sight every so often to see whether you can still recite it correctly simply by visualizing it as if it were there.
- Finally, take all the pieces of paper away and recite the word backwards and forwards by picturing the pieces of paper and the parts of the word.

Putting it all together

Whether you are student or teacher, the ability to recognize your own preferred internal representation enables you to understand what you need to do in order to maximize your performance. Flexibility is key, so teachers need to ensure that they present lessons using all three representational systems – visual, auditory and kinaesthetic – and students can then make the most of what visual materials are used and create their own from what is presented to them in other systems.

(37) Learn in auditory style

> 'Representational systems are also relevant since some tasks are more optimally performed within one representational system than in another. For example, within education, spelling is better learned by clients who have unconsciously used a strategy of visualisation, than an unconscious strategy of phonetically "sounding out".' Terry Elton

> 'The journalist in your head informs you of many things, yet has no real connection to reality as is known in fact.' Terry Elton

> 'Your students with the auditory learning style, about 20 per cent of your class, will also be your social butterflies, so it's important to make good usage of their strengths while dampening their need for social time during a lecture.' Kelly Rowell

> 'If you want to get good rapport, you can speak using the same kind of predicates that the other person is using. If you want to alienate the other person, you can deliberately mismatch predicates.' Richard Bandler and John Grinder

> 'Those able to realize that the thinking of today is about strategy and communication rather than technology alone will be able to run rings around the pure technologists.' Peter Small

Whether as students of teachers, we need to know which internal representation system we naturally prefer, although flexibility is essential because very often we have to adapt to someone's teaching or learning style that doesn't come so easily to us. You are auditory if you prefer to learn by being told rather than reading off a whiteboard or from printed sheets or a book.

People who would describe themselves as auditory enjoy sounds and music but not noise, as they want to control the sounds around them. They enjoy conversation and listening to other people talking, such as radio plays and discussions. What people say is very important to them as well as the way they say it. There are two variations of auditory: **auditory internal** and **auditory digital**. They are both forms of self-talk. The voice behaves like an inner check to sound out whether what someone says is logical or makes sense. It's like having your own personal radio in your head and can enable you to be slightly disassociated or disconnected because you don't directly respond but check out first whether your response is 'correct'. This can be useful in jobs where an emotional or unguarded response could be unwise, such as in the police or teaching.

Auditory learners learn best through spoken lessons, either directly from a teacher in a classroom or via videos, CDs, DVDs MP3 audios, audiobooks and other online learning environments where there is the spoken word. They enjoy learning through discussion as well, so they can assimilate what they've learned. Equally, in the work environment an auditory boss will favour giving oral instructions while an auditory employee will prefer being told what to do rather than receiving an email or text. We want to work in rapport, so match your boss's preferred representational system, and if you are auditory and they are not, ask them to tell you, explain it briefly or let you hear it from them. If they are auditory and you are not, then you'll need to write down what they say so you have a visual record to refer to (if you are visual) or ask them to 'run it by you again' (if you are kinaesthetic).

When communicating with an auditory learner, use words like 'hear', 'listen', 'sound', 'question' and 'resonate'. In order to gain rapport with auditory learners or, indeed, an auditory teacher, speak slowly and choose words carefully. The pitch should match theirs, which will be fairly low with their breathing from the mid-chest. They will look across, not up or down, and construct long sentences with questions because they like to interact.

When you are talking, it may look as though they are thinking about what they want to say next but they are probably just processing what you've said, so leave a silence for them to get their thoughts and the right words together. If you jump into the silence, you will break rapport by not enabling them to contribute to the conversation.

THE AUDITORY TEACHING AND LEARNING STYLE

As an auditory learner, you want to be told rather than shown and you'll find it easier than other students to ask questions and ask for clarification. You can listen and concentrate for much longer than visual or kinaesthetic students, who want to look at things or do things as part of their learning preference.

When you read, especially as a young child, you'll have sounded out the words and may even do that sometimes now if you read a particularly complex sentence or some very beautiful-sounding writing. You'll spell phonetically, sounding out as you do so. You may find that you need to learn visually in order to spell words that are not phonetic. Do this by writing them out, breaking the word into small chunks and then practising each bit by looking at the letters, taking the paper away and saying what they are. When you can do that backwards, then you know you are learning visually.

Words like 'hear', 'listen', 'sound' and 'question' will ring true for you, so, if you are a teacher, as well as telling auditory students what you want them to learn, spell it out for them so they are clear. If you hand out visual material, it will help communicate complex concepts if you choose the auditory learners to read out a paragraph each. Meanwhile, the visual learners can read it to themselves.

If you're auditory internal or auditory digital, you will want to process what you've learned and consider it, understand it and think about it.

Using mnemonics and word association will help you remember facts for tests, as will repeating facts with your eyes closed. After you have written your notes, read them out and record them on an MP3 so that you can listen to them at every opportunity. You will enjoy making up rhymes or songs to remember things, and reading out loud will also be a good revision technique. Some auditory learners benefit from playing classical music in the background when they are studying. Others like to be asked test questions for them to answer out loud and others like to discuss the content of their studies.

If you are teaching auditory learners, be sure to slow down and speak slowly and carefully. Put auditory learners near the front of the class and offer students the opportunity to tape your lesson so they can listen back later. Ask them to read out sections of the lesson material, and organize ways that they can be involved in paired activities and projects – the 20 per cent of your class who learn in an auditory style, together with your kinaesthetic learners, will form half the class, a half that needs to be actively doing something rather than just watching and reading.

PARENTING AN AUDITORY CHILD

You will know if your child is auditory because they probably talk a lot, enjoy singing and listening to music and making a noise. They will be quite chatty and enjoy asking questions in order to engage you in conversation. When you read to them, they will want to make the noises of the characters and ask you about them. They will learn from hearing you use words and you'll soon find them repeating them for themselves, so they will have a good spoken vocabulary, even though they may not recognize the words when they see them in written form.

You may need to read out homework questions to help them focus, and to ask them what they think the answer is, because they will more confidently tell you than write it down. When they learn spellings, help them to break the word down into sound chunks and start introducing visual learning (remember, not all words are phonetic). Do this by writing out each spelling and asking them to look at it. Then take the word away and ask them to read out the letters backwards (this shows they are learning visually rather than remembering auditorily). When you start this at an early age with short words like 'cat' (with images to help them), they will get into the habit and be able to apply the same technique to longer words and words without images. When they have reading homework, they will prefer to read out loud to you rather than to themselves. Give them audiobooks to encourage them to 'read' more complex books than they could tackle visually.

Times tables can be learned through songs and rhymes, which are readily available.

Be careful of shouting at auditory children because this will disturb them more than a visual child because they are so aware of sound. They will note the words you use and remember them, so they will also be easily hurt by unkind words from siblings or thoughtless comments made by teachers or parents.

KNOWING IF YOU ARE AUDITORY

The chances are that you like talking and conversation. You are happy to chat on the phone for ages and relish a good natter with a friend. You enjoy music and are musical, but when music is on you want to listen to it and enjoy it rather than having it play in the background. In fact, discordant or loud music may offend you if it isn't your own choice. You'll easily be distracted by 'sounds off' that are outside your control such as a dripping tap or squeaky door, other people's phone conversations and noisy kids.

The chances are that you speak slowly, choosing your words with care because you want to be sure to convey what you intend, and that you also listen carefully, often remembering what was said word for word. You enjoy discussion and asking questions and listening to the explanations. You tend to follow instructions well and remember what you've been told. You can't keep quiet for long periods and enjoy interacting with others. You like presenting and being given the opportunity to speak or act.

You'll be good at learning to speak languages and you'll pick up accents quickly because you will hear the way the other person sounds out the words and be able to copy it. You'll also remember grammar rules because they'll sound right or wrong to you immediately. Therefore, you'll be good at oral exams.

Where the visual person will tend to raise their eye level, looking up to access pictures from their brain, auditory people are more likely to move their eyes sideways. You breathe from lower down in your chest and your voice will have a lower pitch than a visual person's.

Putting it all together

If you process as an auditory person, you will be very sociable and chatty, people will enjoy your company and you'll be more comfortable in company than most. You won't necessarily enjoy an open-plan office, though, because extraneous noise will be distracting, so get some music on those headphones. This will also be true for students in a classroom, so place auditory learners at the front where they can hear you better and where there will be fewer distractions. Auditory students take advantage of every opportunity to learn through hearing and transfer visual into auditory whenever possible.

Learn in kinaesthetic style

❝ 'When people are like each other they like each other.' Terry Elston

❝ 'If they are kinaesthetic, slow waaay dooown. Talk to them about feelings. Change your pace so that it matches theirs, and really get a feel for what they are communicating.' Terry Elston

❝ 'What I hear, I forget. What I see, I remember. What I do, I understand.' Confucius

❝ 'In many ways, touch is the most immediate of the senses. It brings you "into contact" with the world. We say that "seeing is believing" but, for many people, touching makes it real.' Joseph O'Connor

❝ 'Those with a kinaesthetic preference often require more time to consider a situation as they need to calculate how they feel about things and this takes longer than simply creating a picture in their mind.' Jeff Archer

Kinaesthetic people learn by doing; they need to physically experience the learning because they are active full-body learners. You'll see them fidgeting in classrooms when they have to sit still for long periods and they need to take a break regularly to run about and stretch. They're usually quite sporty and in touch with their body and how it feels, so they will be quite tactile and sensitive to the heat and cold. They will also be quite expressive.

Research conducted as long ago as 1980 by Brockman into the effects of matching internal representational systems (VAK)

concluded that matched clients preferred the counsellor (in this example) by a ratio of 3:1 compared to counsellors who didn't match and used a more generic teaching style. If applied to teaching, this suggests that by matching you will improve your connection and rapport with your students threefold.

Characteristics of kinaesthetic people are that they will be active speakers and listeners and use facial expression, hand and body gestures and will fiddle and fidget when talking rather than adopting the stiller pose of the auditory student. They refer to their 'gut feelings' and 'being in touch' with their feelings and may respond more emotionally to events than one might expect. Comfort and body temperature are important to them, so extremes of heat and cold are not endured easily. It is important to them to be comfortable in their own skin, and to wear clothes that are comfortable rather than ones that look good (visual). Furniture is also bought for comfort rather than style.

They want to get 'stuck in' and do rather than watch or be told. It's all about involvement, both physical and mental. Given a new piece of equipment, rather than read the instructions they'll just work it out for themselves by trial and error. They will get themselves from A to B by what feels like the right route rather than read a map or listen to the satnav. They will be conscious of atmosphere and want to be in rapport because not to be would feel so uncomfortable.

Physically, they are very active and will want to stand much closer to you than you may be comfortable with, but don't move away as this will break rapport. They may want to touch your elbow or arm as you're chatting and they will probably hug and kiss on greeting and leaving. They talk slowly, even more slowly than an auditory person, and tend to look down as they speak as they get in touch with their emotions. Their choice of words will reflect their action and feelings orientation, so expect to hear words like 'feel', 'touch', 'get hold of', 'catch on to', 'get a handle on' and 'make contact with'. If you work with a kinaesthetic person or have one as a client, you'll find that they want to meet up physically as opposed to emailing or making conference calls and that they will do business on the golf course or squash court rather than in a meeting room.

THE KINAESTHETIC TEACHING AND LEARNING STYLE

Kinaesthetic learners learn by moving, touching and doing. Hands-on learning is what they like best, actively exploring the world around them. They will remember well what they have done but will have trouble remembering what was said or seen. Fiddling is second nature, as is doodling – why do one thing when you can do two? They'll have trouble sitting still in a classroom, so plenty of active breaks are needed as well as opportunities to move about through class activities such as group work or practical activities.

As a kinaesthetic student, you may not be able to control your classroom environment or ask for breaks but there are things you can do to aid your learning. Use coloured highlighters to mark up your notes and use mind maps to transfer information into a form that makes it easier to remember.

When you have subject choices, choose subjects that are more practical or those that have practical elements such as Geography (with field trips), Science, Drama, Sport and Design and Technology. At home, when revising or doing homework, use flash cards or memory games and interactive programs on the computer in order to make the most of the material. Many computer-based revision programs offer multiple-choice questions and these will suit you.

TASTE AND SMELL

There are two other senses that are generally considered to be part of the kinaesthetic internal representational system. These are the olfactory and gustatory systems.

Olfactory relates to smell. Our sense of smell is very powerful and can conjure up some strong positive and negative emotions. Think about smells that remind you of happy times, your childhood perhaps. Mothers often love the smell of newborn babies or baby creams that remind them of this special time in their life. Many people love the smell of freshly mown grass; others like the smell of an open fire, hay, blossom, flowers and, of course, food. Many vegetarians comment that they are sometimes tempted by the smell of bacon frying. Then there are smells that have negative associations such as the smell of toilets or body odour. Smell can be a powerful unconscious anchor when a smell reminds us of something and we get mentally transported to that time or place without being aware of it.

Gustatory relates to taste and this, too, can form powerful associations in our minds and positive and negative unconscious anchors, and can create experiences from which we can learn, although this will be more acute for those in the cooking profession.

Although in the Western world these two elements of the kinaesthetic internal representational system are less relevant to most students as a learning style, they are generally considered to be part of it and can be more relevant in other cultures.

HOW TO DEVELOP YOUR KINAESTHETIC LEARNING

Much emphasis is placed on learning by seeing and hearing, but when you can involve all three senses you get a richer experience:

Get in touch with your kinaesthetic learning style by first becoming bodily aware. Do this by allowing your mind to travel through your body from head to toe, making yourself aware of every part. Flex and stretch each muscle and notice how it moves, how flexible it is and what it can do. Can you make it move more by asking it to? You can.

Secondly, experiment with touch and explore how your body feels on the outside. Which parts feel softer and which rougher? Where are you ticklish? How does it change when you press more firmly and then very gently? Now touch other surfaces around you. How do they feel?

Thirdly, experiment with balance. Stand on both feet and notice whether you are completely upright or whether you lean slightly. Check with a mirror or ask someone. Rock backwards and forwards on your feet until you're sure that you have your weight firmly in the middle. Next, balance on one foot and then the other, noticing how looking up, then down and then straight ahead affects how well you can balance.

Lastly, become aware of how you are feeling. What words or pictures come to mind that would describe you at the moment? Owning our emotions gives us choices about what to do with them.

Putting it all together

We all have elements of visual, auditory and kinaesthetic internal representational systems but, whereas visual and auditory are generally pretty well catered for in schools, kinaesthetic learners can find long lessons with few breaks and a lot of writing and listening very difficult to manage. They need to be doing something. Sometimes they can even be diagnosed as having learning difficulties despite the fact that when doing something active they can be very focused and engaged. Teachers need to be aware of different learning styles and cater for those who need frequent breaks and more interactive learning. Equally, however, kinaesthetic learners need to consider how they can make what is offered as involving as they can.

39 Use 'big chunk' and 'small chunk' processing at work

 'So what's the answer to keep everyone happy? In simple terms it's teaching individuals a way of chunking information so they can deliver it in a way that's appropriate for the listener. So if you're a "specific" person I'd teach you how to give an overview first and then provide details to back up the information if required. The overview is like a filing cabinet into which the details (the individual files) can be located. If you're a "global" person I would teach you to chunk down and provide sufficient detailed, sensory information. Information that relates specifically to the person who will be carrying out the task.' Stephanie Philp

 'Don't opt for small or big chunks but right-sized chunks, the right size for you.' Harry Adler

 'The way we communicate with others and with ourselves ultimately determines the quality of our lives.' Tony Robbins

 'In NLP the idea of chunking up or down is used extensively. Questions are asked to elicit the next level of information and bring about a new way of perceiving a situation. For instance, to chunk up, a useful question to ask might be "what is that an example of?" To chunk down, ask "what would be an example of this?"' Steve Bavister and Amanda Vickers

 'The ability to chunk up and down is an ability of excellent negotiators.' Sue Knight

Rapport, the way we get on with people, can be enhanced when we match the way they process information because in that way it appears that we are 'speaking the same language'. Processing information refers both to the way we convey what we want to say ourselves and how we like to receive information given by others. **Big chunk** describes vague, big picture or concept-type thinking, while **small chunk** refers to detailed information. Which is your preference?

Big chunk/small chunk is a continuum or scale along which we all fall in terms of how we like our information presented and how we like to communicate our own. At the extreme end, the smallest chunk information would be extremely detailed and what some might call 'nit-picky'. Someone with small chunk skills would make an excellent proofreader, book-keeper or contract checker because they would work through the detail, spotting inconsistencies and mistakes. A person with big chunk skills would be good at coming up with ideas and new concepts, and able to imagine global perspectives and business objectives. They could come across as vague and unclear because they don't 'join up the dots' and leave others to work out what they mean. Some jobs and some tasks obviously require us to operate big chunk and other jobs require our detailed attention, so ideally we need both sets of skills. However, we may have a natural inclination to one end or the other of the scale, even though we may be required to be flexible. In fact, the more flexible we can be the better, as it opens up more choices.

This flexibility comes into play when giving instructions because you may be inclined to give someone more detail than they find they can handle and they zone out halfway through because, once they've got the general idea, they lose interest in the details. That would be a big chunk person. Or you might give them the general gist and leave them to work out the detail. That might be fine for a big chunk processor, but the small chunk processor will still be standing there wondering when you're going to brief them properly.

We need to be able to slide up and down the scale because, when setting objectives or devising a plan, we need to have access to big chunk thinking rather than getting bogged down in the detail, but when it comes to implementing the plan, detail is key. If you find it difficult to have that flexibility, then make sure that you have people on your team who have those skills.

We can see how chunk size is used in report writing, with an executive summary for higher management and small chunk in the body of the report for those who have to implement it. In learning, new topics are treated big chunk when they are introduced and then the trainer or teacher will drill down into the detail to explore the topic in depth.

CHUNKING UP

This is the term we give to the action of sliding up the scale and becoming bigger chunk. We do it and encourage others to do it when it appears they are getting bogged down in detail. It can be difficult to get agreement on a general course of action when parties to the decision are getting embroiled in detail. By chunking up, you can find common ground and connections, areas of general agreement to work from.

The movement can sometimes be prompted by someone saying, 'So what does this mean?' or 'What is that an example of?' or 'What's the purpose of…?' in order to draw conclusions and elicit a broader meaning from the information.

Chunking up is used for conflict resolution in order to find common ground at a higher or purpose level, rather than arguing over fine points of principle. It is also used to set goals because people are not usually inspired by small chunk goals such as passing this exam but chunk up to what passing this exam will mean in the future – the possibility of going to college, getting a great job, earning lots of money and having a great lifestyle.

Similarly, if you're getting bored with study or doing the daily grind of a not very inspiring job, practising your scales on the piano or declensions of verbs, think instead of what doing this will bring you in the future – the ability to play Mozart on the piano, get a job abroad or whatever is your passion.

When we want alternative courses of action and think laterally, it helps to chunk up to look at options on a broader canvas.

The ability to chunk up in negotiations moves things towards consensus.

CHUNKING DOWN

Going in the other direction, we collect information and move away from concept thinking. This is where you'll find the detail and the action plan, the 'to do' list and allocation of tasks. Every organization needs people doing things while others do the 'blue sky' thinking and come up with new ideas. We need small chunk people to check facts, order stock, check quality control, ascertain legal requirements, complete shipping forms, order envelopes and so on..

When you want to chunk someone down to get specific details, you need to ask questions such as 'How will we do that specifically?', 'Can you give me specific examples of this?', 'How do we know this?' and 'What is the deadline?'

Chunking down is used in learning in order to group related facts into pockets to learn together (e.g. mind maps or bullet points). Using mnemonics helps students remember specifics to ensure that they cover all the detailed points once they've written the initial overview.

When someone is feeling overwhelmed or depressed and finds themselves saying things like 'I can't cope', 'I'm always shouting at the kids' or 'I never meet deadlines', these generalizations can seem much more manageable when they chunk down to precisely what they are having a problem with, which deadline they are having trouble meeting, or exactly when they shout. Having to be specific enables them to adjust their perception and be more reasonable about what's happening. Things aren't really so bad when you chunk down in those situations.

CHUNKING FOR RAPPORT

Imagine you are communicating with someone who loves detail and you are talking in the abstract; they would get really frustrated and want to pin you down to facts and figures. Similarly, if you were giving someone all the detailed research background and taking ages and they'd only asked you a quick broad-brush question about when the new product was coming out, you'd soon see them looking at their watch and finding a pressing need to be elsewhere. It's important to recognize what chunk size to answer with or to open with, and you can do this by either asking the direct question 'How much detail do you want?' or some other phrase such as 'Do you want the long answer or the short one?' or 'How long have you got?' All these are common ways of dealing with this issue.

Putting it all together

Organizations, families and schools all need people who can manage big chunk and small chunk processing, and if you can do both then you are at a distinct advantage, especially if you can accurately gauge which is needed when. Learn to recognize when you're using what size chunk and exercise your skills by taking it up or down a chunk, just to see how much flexibility you can acquire. Remember, the person with the most flexibility controls the system.

40 Give or make a choice where there is none

'Having just one choice is no choice at all. The more choices you have, the more freedom you have to be in the driving seat of your car.' Steve Bavister

'The whole point of NLP is having more choice.' Richard Bandler

'You're not just a leaf on the wind.' Tony Robbins

'We are making hundreds, thousands, even millions of unconscious choices every day about what we pay attention to and what we don't. And this is fine, provided those choices work for us. However, if we are not getting the results we want, we can learn to make new choices until we find what does work.' Sue Knight

'Identifying, acknowledging, examining, and employing our parts, rules, and inner wisdom help us transform our internal process and deal with present circumstances. By removing our self-made limits, we expand our choices.' Virginia Satir

Some people thrive on choice and enjoy the element of selecting from a number of options, whether it be what to wear, what to buy, what to cook or eat, or even what to say, but others prefer to just pick something and go with it. In NLP terms, we call it **choices** or **process**, the latter indicating that those who don't like choices want to work their way down a list of tasks as a process rather than branching off or pausing to make decisions. It isn't really a bipolar scale; these are just the two ends of it.

There may be situations in which you want choice, when you go out for a meal perhaps or when buying clothes, but in the rush of the morning you may prefer not to spend ages choosing what to wear or what to eat for breakfast. This means that you will be sliding up and down the scale depending on the situation. However, being aware of whether you want a choice or not can be helpful. If, as you think about the situation presenting itself, you decide whether choices will help or hinder the process, you will work more efficiently. This is particularly the case when working with others.

In a work situation, decide first whether or not your colleague or employee has a choice and, if they do, what these choices are. Also, decide what they are *not*. For example, they may have a choice how to perform a task but not whether or not to perform it. They may have the choice whether to do it on Wednesday or Thursday, but not whether they can do it next week. Make it clear what choices are available.

In a family situation, it is very important to make clear to your children what are options and what are not. There has been a growing trend to encourage children to make choices, even at a very young age, whether to drink out of a red mug or a blue one, whether to wear this or that dress. This is inclined to make children capricious, as they assume they can make decisions about everything, which isn't of course the case and can lead to some very lengthy preparations for leaving the house! You need to prepare your children for accepting your decisions and make it clear when they can choose and when it isn't possible or appropriate. You can signal this by asking, 'Would you like to choose?' when there is a choice.

It is useful to know whether the person you are talking to likes choices or not in each situation because you will have greater rapport if you give choices to someone who wants them and not to someone who doesn't. In a work context, you can appear to give choice if someone wants that by offering choices between a number of options, all of which are acceptable to you. If someone doesn't want choices, you just give them instructions on what needs to be done and by when.

In the family, you would similarly offer false choices to children who want choice — for example, 'Would you like to do your homework with a cup of tea or a glass of milk?' Note that not doing homework wasn't an option! Also, with 'like' and 'homework' close together in the sentence you are giving them a slightly hypnotic connection that might not have been present for them.

CHOICE PEOPLE VS. PROCESS PEOPLE

When someone who likes choices is talking with someone who doesn't it is difficult to get rapport. The person who likes choices enjoys deliberating and considering all the options. Maybe they are perusing the menu wondering what to have. You've decided, but they weigh up the appeal of the chicken versus the duck, which vegetables, chips or sauté potatoes, and so on. It can be maddening. For one person, the pleasure is in the selection and for the other it is all about just getting the task done so they can move on to another.

In another situation, you may be the person who likes choices while the other doesn't – it can be very annoying, for example, shopping with someone who doesn't. You want to discuss which colours and textures you like, whether to go for a dress or a blouse and skirt, which colour, which shop and so on, and all they want to do is tick things off their list as they shop.

It can be tempting, when there is a mismatch, for the process person to hurry the choices person by helping them to make the choice, even going so far as to choose for them, but this won't be appreciated. Similarly, choices people like to introduce choice to process people. Desist – they don't want it! If they ask for tea, just give the tea – don't go suggesting hundreds of different types.

Importantly for rapport, you need to be sensitive to the other person and be aware of whether they want choice or process.

DISCOVERING CHOICES

Sometimes we find ourselves in situations where there appears to be no choice. You may have to sit next to someone you can't stand, give bad news to the Board, finish a relationship that has become dysfunctional, put down a loved pet that is suffering.

You know it has to be done and there appears to be no choice. However, be curious and you will discover choices. If you like choices or feel stressed by the lack of them, then think about the choices you have even in these situations or other similar ones. You can choose what to talk about with the person next to you, decide how to give the bad news, and so on. You may not have the choice about the 'what' but you have the choice about 'how'. The first part of the choice element is choosing to communicate in rapport by matching the behaviour and voice tone and style of the other person and then the language patterns. Once you are in rapport, things will flow more easily and you'll soon find yourself managing the situation in a resourceful manner.

THERE IS ALWAYS A CHOICE

Parents need to know how to give choice when there is none because offering choices is not always an option when you want your children to get dressed to go to school by a certain time, eat healthy meals or do their homework. If you have older children, you may not want to give them choices about what time to come home or where they go and with whom.

First, decide on your compelling outcome. What end result do you want from the discussion or negotiation? What will you concede and what is non-negotiable? Simply going through this process has a remarkably calming effect and puts you in the driving seat. If, for example, the pick-up time is non-negotiable, you can give them a choice of how they come home, with whom and by what means of transport. If the time you have to leave for the school run is non-negotiable, give them a choice about getting dressed before or after breakfast, whether to wear a jumper or not, or whether they need to give their shoes a clean.

There is always a choice, not just in terms of the 'how' but also in how you ask. You can speak in rapport, using your child's preferred language pattern – visual, auditory or kinaesthetic. If they are talking about what they don't want (e.g. 'I don't want to put on my shirt'), mention something you don't want in order to match them ('and I don't want to be late for the bus'). If they say, 'Yes, but…' or 'no', this is a mismatch pattern that you can still match for rapport by using the same pattern – 'Yes, but homework needs to be done first' or 'No, it has to be done first, then TV.'

Learning about NLP means that we have choices based on more knowledge about ourselves and how we see our world and a better understanding of the other person's world. We can then choose how we want to communicate with them.

Putting it all together

Even when there appears to be no choice in the 'what' that we have to do, there is always a choice in the 'how'. There is a choice also in how we communicate, what we choose to believe about a situation and a choice in how we frame it. We can use anchoring to choose our most resourceful state and we can choose to communicate in rapport. These choices give us flexibility, which puts us in control if we choose to be.

41

Know where you are – past, present or future

> 'The connections we make and the way we represent memories, ideas and information are unique to each one of us. Everyone has their own way of thinking. When we understand the nature of our representations, we begin to influence our thinking, our emotions and consequently our experience. What we think is what we are.' Sue Knight

> 'The best thing about the past is that it's over. The best thing about the future is that it's yet to come. The best thing about the present is that it's here now.' Richard Bandler

> 'Memories are myths.' Tony Robbins

> 'We all have beliefs and expectations from our personal experience; it is impossible to live without them. Since we have to make some assumptions, they might as well be ones that allow us freedom, choice and fun in the world, rather than ones that limit us. You often get what you expect to get.' John Seymour

> 'Free your expectation of the future from the grip of past failure.' John Seymour

We are often told that we should live 'in the moment'. However, having the flexibility to time-travel and access our past and future as well as the present can give us options that will enable us to bring skills to the present from our past and foresee a time when we will be happier (if, for example, we are grieving and anxious) as well as being able to fully appreciate the moment (or not, if it is unpleasant).

When we place ourselves in the past, this can be a stuck place where we haven't moved on in our life. Perhaps we hold on to fears and anxieties and limiting beliefs from our youth instead of accepting that we may have outgrown them and can move on. When we talk about past events as though they were still true today, we are limiting our opportunities to change and develop. The only way to be confident is to push yourself out of your comfort area of the past and things with which you are familiar and enter new ground with new possibilities. These old anxieties are based on old beliefs, and just as we have outgrown our belief in the tooth fairy and in Father Christmas, maybe it's also time to change our beliefs about our fears and limitations.

A problem we sometimes encounter when trying to do this is that we generalize. We cannot remember perhaps the specific incident or precise thing we couldn't do, so we generalize. Thus, an anxiety about one particular maths problem can become 'I always struggle with numbers' and we avoid that promotion because it will involve finance or accounting. A problem in the past with a dog can morph into a phobia of dogs, even though you may not even remember the details of what happened. Perhaps you heard your parent remark that you were scared of dogs or that you found maths difficult and this endorsement from an adult of great influence at that age can become a belief you carry forward through your life.

When we focus on the past and the present, the future becomes hazy territory which we avoid visiting despite the fact that, if we do not consider the future, it is hard to know where we are heading. This is often a problem for young people, so fixated on today's school pressures to pass this exam or that one, with little thought as to where these exams lead beyond the next step in the education path. It can happen that they get to a crisis point when their motivation and commitment to the process fail and they ask themselves 'What's it all for?' Little thought is given at school to what young people are working towards. Quite often, the focus is 'away from': 'Work hard, otherwise you won't get a job.' We all get into 'stuck' places where we can't do something – lose weight, get on with our partner, manage our kids or get on with the boss – but when we can't see forward into the future there seems to be no solution. Sometimes the solution may be in the past. For example, what did you do last time something like this happened? What was the solution then? Could that work now? Or the solution may be in the future in terms of how we'd like it to be. Once we can visualize what we want, we are on the way to getting it.

CHANGING PERSONAL HISTORY

Our thoughts and feelings about the past and the future have a powerful effect on how we feel in the present, so how would it be if we could change those beliefs and perceptions? These are not set in stone and, in fact, two people can have different memories about the same event. We can't change what happened but we can use our present knowledge and understanding to change the way the past affects our present and future.

Close your eyes and take yourself back to the time when you experienced the feeling that is causing you a problem now. It could be around a particular event that was frightening or upsetting, but imagine it is happening now as you focus on it and experience it. Notice what you saw then, what you heard and let your whole body experience what you felt. Is this the first time you experienced this feeling? If not, travel back in time to the first time you experienced it. It may have been a different event, so repeat the procedure and imagine it is happening now. Now anchor this unresourceful feeling by squeezing your left earlobe.

Shake yourself off and think about what resources or states you have now that would have been useful then. Focus on these skills and resources as you anchor them. Do this by reminding yourself of times in the present when you have used that resource and, as you concentrate on that occasion, squeeze your right earlobe (because you want to anchor in a different place).

Shake yourself off again. Now, let's test the new anchor by going back to the past event and use this new anchor for the new resource, so squeeze your right earlobe. Notice how everything is different now that you have this new resource.

Now, let's imagine a similar event that you expect to happen in the future and use this new anchor and notice how different it will be, now that you have changed your personal history. With this exercise, we can release ourselves from negative emotions and limiting beliefs in order to have the future we want to have.

WHERE ARE YOU IN TIME?

Are you someone who lives in the past, thinking back to happier times, a bit nostalgic perhaps? It's not only old people who do this. Lots of mothers think back fondly of the time when their children were little. Couples remember when they were in love; teenagers remember how much simpler life was when they were younger; and unconscious anchors such as smells and tastes can transport us to a younger age in an instant. Or are you someone who constantly thinks of what you're going to do tomorrow or next week? How often do you live in the moment, experiencing each hour of the day as it happens? It's good to be able to access each of these time zones, and especially the present, so here are a few questions to bring you into the present:

- What are you doing right now?
- How do you feel this minute?
- What is that like?
- What else is true for you now?

We can let the past limit us or we can let it go. Many people who are trying to lose weight, give up smoking or leave an abusive partner can feel stuck in the past because they have 'always' smoked or 'always 'been overweight or 'always' allowed people to take advantage of them. They have let these experiences become their present identity, so even as they lose weight, stand up for themselves or cut down their smoking, it doesn't 'feel' right because they are living with how they were. If you are making a change in your life, ask yourself 'Who am I now?' and 'How does this new person want to behave?'

Similarly, if you are going to lose weight, quit your job or quit smoking, work harder, tomorrow or next week, ask yourself 'And what could I do about that today?'

Living in the present with access to the past for resources and the future for opportunities and possibilities gives you options.

DO YOU DELETE, DISTORT OR GENERALIZE TIME?

Deletions occur when you remember only certain aspects of the past, so perhaps when you think back on the early days of your relationship and think you were happy then, you may be deleting those times when you were not. We may look back at our first job and think we hated it, but again perhaps we are remembering some negative aspects but deleting many positive ones.

Distortions occur when we make an assumption based on value judgements, cause and effect, or interpretations. Examples would be saying that 'going to a certain school meant that you didn't get a good job' or that your parents made you feel inadequate. We are making assumptions based on flimsy evidence.

Examples of generalizations are saying 'always' and 'never' or using limiters such as saying 'I can't…' or 'I must…' These are, like deletions and distortions, almost never true.

If you suspect you might be deleting, distorting or generalizing, ask yourself whether there could be another way to frame what happened by imagining how someone else who was not there and not involved might interpret it.

Putting it all together

Once you know where you are at any time, you can bring yourself back to the present and focus on what's happening right now and what you can do to ensure that you take into the future only positive and resourceful memories. You can also learn from memories that are less positive, and bring that learning into the present and into the future.

42 Know when to match – and when to mismatch

"" *'The key to mismatching is in the phrase: "yes, but…" This phrase challenges the other person to think, to re-examine their presuppositions and their entrenched positions. It can lead to arguments and disagreements. But it can also cause a lot of rethinking and re-evaluating which can be healthy.'*
David Ferrers

"" *'The key to establishing rapport is an ability to enter another person's world by assuming a similar state of mind. The first thing to do is to become more like the other person by matching and mirroring the person's behaviours – body language, voice, words, etc. Matching and mirroring is a powerful way of getting an appreciation of how the other person is seeing/experiencing the world.'* Roger Ellerton

"" *'A mismatching frame can be a very creative filter to put on, particularly if the task needs a revolutionary approach. Entrepreneurs are often the people who see how things can be different. It is great when you need a critic or devil's advocate.'* Kim Davis

"" *'Every team needs at least one mismatcher. They will point out new directions.'* Ian McDermott

"" *'First you have to have fun. Second you have to put love where your labour is. Third you have to go in the opposite direction to everyone else.'* Anita Roddick

Matching is when we copy what the person we are with is doing and saying, but not exactly because that would look ridiculous and would not be liked at all. It is about agreeing and being agreeable and looking for what we have in common with the other person. When we match, we look for common ground, things we like; **mismatching** is doing the opposite. In fact, when you watch people who are in a well-established relationship they will appear to mirror each other. Having learned that, we should be aiming to match for rapport, there are times when the ability to mismatch could be useful.

Examples of matching are when we meet someone new and look for what we have in common, such as living in the same area, doing a similar job, having children the same age and so on. Matching skills are invaluable for making friends. When children move on to secondary school or the next grade, we encourage them by reminding them who they already know and what will be similar so they aren't overwhelmed. At a party, we seek out people who look as if they could be similar to us in age or type of clothes, which might indicate that we will have something in common. Clubs tend to attract people who have interests or sports in common, and that's often a good basis for forming friendships such as walking clubs, golf and tennis.

If you have a job in sales, you know that people buy from people they like and trust, so matching creates rapport and an ambiance of trust and friendship where people are willing to buy, do business and commission work. As soon as someone says, 'Yes, but…', there is a disconnect, a mismatch and our hackles rise, as we wonder what challenge will occur to rock the gentle status quo. When we start a new job, we generally feel more comfortable if systems are similar, so we can carry over our knowledge and processes. When we meet new colleagues, they will try to think of people they know from your old company and people you might already know at the new one. It's the most natural way to seek agreement and common ground, to match. It's how people connect and have rapport-ful relationships.

However, a matching conversation can go on for ever and sometimes there is a need to move on to another subject, get things done or leave. You may need to resolve a situation, find an answer to a problem or look at a situation from another angle, and in these sorts of situations a mismatch will change the dynamics and allow another path to be taken that might in some circumstances be resourceful. For example, if everyone is in total agreement to take action A but action A is not an option, the only way to get them to think about other possibilities will be to introduce a mismatch – for example, 'Well, I think Option B does have some merits' – and this will stop the matching process and get people to address this possibility. This will be essential if you are talking with a depressed person because when you match you will feel their depression and won't be able to lift their mood unless you mismatch. Also, if someone is being very argumentative and you are enjoying a good argument as you match, you will need to start mismatching by agreeing with them if you want to stop. Youngsters all matching an undesirable course of action will need someone to mismatch in order to keep the group safe or to avoid group peer pressure. Extreme matchers can be so resistant to change that they will stay with a bad crowd or a bad relationship rather than risk change by mismatching.

HOW TO START MATCHING

Because body language is such an important aspect of rapport, this is the best starting point when matching. When you first meet someone, their impression of you is based 55 per cent on your body language, 38 per cent on your voice and only 7 per cent on what you say. Therefore the easiest way to start establishing rapport is by matching the other person's body language. If they are sitting, draw up a chair and sit next to them, or if you can't, then squat down so your heads are roughly at the same height. This is extremely important when you want to build rapport with children and those in a wheelchair. If the other person is standing, then stand up.

Once you are on the same level, it will be easier to make eye contact, which is a key ingredient of rapport. Match their eye contact, though, because some people prefer minimal eye contact and others more, so notice how much eye contact they are inviting.

Matching your breathing is another powerful way to connect, although one would caution against eyeballing the other person's chest. If they are using hand gestures, do the same, although you should avoid using exactly the same gesture — simply move your hands so you also seem animated.

Next, move on to matching the voice. The most obvious aspects are speed and pitch, so, if they are talking faster than you, speed up; and if they are talking in a higher pitch, raise yours a bit to match them. These aspects would indicate that they might be visual people, because this type tends to speak quickly as they access images from their head.

Match the visual person by using words like 'look', 'see', 'watch' and other words that indicate a focus on what can be seen. Match the auditory person, who may speak slowly and carefully, by doing the same and using words like 'hear', 'listen' and 'speak'. The kinaesthetic person may gesture a lot and talk quickly, fidgeting perhaps. They tend to use doing and feeling words like 'get', 'do' and 'run'.

Whatever words they use, match them because these are the words they like. When you use those words, too, they will like you because they'll recognize a kindred spirit.

HOW TO INTRODUCE A MISMATCH

There are a number of reasons why you might want to mismatch, as was mentioned earlier, but how can you do this seamlessly? Assuming you've done a really good job of matching, you only need a minor mismatch to make a difference.

- The easiest one is to break eye contact by pointing something out or checking your phone, or by standing up if you're both sitting down.
- You can also introduce the 'Yes, but…' mismatching pattern.
- You can point out what is different about what they are saying, describing it as 'unique' or 'a new way of thinking'.
- You could disagree and bring out the evidence by saying, 'But research shows…'

If you are communicating with a matcher who looks for what is the same but you want them to change their behaviour and do something different, then, instead of mentioning how different the new behaviour is, talk about the ways in which it is the same. With a mismatcher you would point out what is different.

In situations where matching has created a really good rapport but no new thinking or alternatives, then you will need to mismatch.

MISMATCHING AND TEENAGERS

It seems almost a rite of passage for teenagers to mismatch in order to free themselves of the umbilical cord. One minute they're behaving apparently quite normally and the next, everything you say is wrong and they want to do the opposite of whatever you've suggested. You have two options: to match or mismatch.

Matching is nearly always the better option as it keeps you and your teenager in rapport. When we mismatch, we simply perpetuate the argument and make it more difficult to resolve. So avoid 'Yes, but…' as this is classic mismatching and avoid 'no' as this is also basic mismatching.

You want to match for rapport and because you love them. However, you want a different result, so here are some options:

- You can suggest they don't want to do something that you want them to do: 'I know you won't want to revise for your exam / come home earlier and when you do you will…' To mismatch, they now have to revise or come home earlier. Instead of using 'if', indicating that there is a choice about it, you have used 'when', which assumes compliance. Replacing 'but' with 'and' keeps you in rapport and evens up the emphasis of the sentence whereas a 'but' tends to emphasize everything after it.
- Leave articles or books around that you want them to read rather than suggesting they read them and assume the mismatch.
- When they are looking for differences, you can match by saying, 'That's a really unusual idea and I'm wondering how we can make it work' or 'That's a very new way of thinking about… and I'll certainly give it some consideration.' Point out differences such as 'All your friends' mums say they have started their revision but I expect they haven't.'

There are obviously some areas where you would not want to give mixed messages such as those to do with alcohol, sex and drugs, violence and so on. Here, you need to have a consistent and strong message and give them clear boundaries. This is what they expect and, while it's fine to match their mismatch on relatively trivial things, it is not OK on these important issues.

Putting it all together

In most situations, we want rapport because that is the way we make connections and form lasting relationships. In order to establish and hold rapport, we need to match body language, voice tones and pace and types of language (visual, auditory and kinaesthetic). In that way, we respectfully enter another's world and see it as they see it, which helps in understanding them. However, we have the choice to match or mismatch, and sometimes the choice to mismatch will produce a solution that can come about only by challenging the status quo. Also, when matching with a mismatcher, it is essential that we know the tricks of mismatching.

43 Use the power of disassociation

'Disassociation is a useful technique if you want to put some distance between yourself and a memory. As a general rule, think of your pleasant memories in an associated way to get the most enjoyment from them and your uncomfortable memories in a disassociated way to avoid the bad feelings.'
Joseph O'Connor

'We all have the temptation sometimes to take the emotions of the present and apply them to our thoughts for the future which can limit our positivity or creativity. Where this is a possibility, you can use the technique of disassociation to ensure you judge the future with a clear head and without any limitation that may be part of your current situation.' Jeff Archer

'The objectivity we get from standing back or taking a helicopter view can be extremely valuable. When we're in a situation our emotions can get in the way of noticing what's going on, particularly when there's conflict or aggressive behaviour. Third position is also called the "meta" position and features in many NLP patterns and change techniques providing an opportunity for the person to stand outside their own experience when that's required.' Steve Bavister and Amanda Vickers

'The only way to get the best of an argument is to avoid it.'
Dale Carnegie

To **disassociate** is to separate ourselves from the emotions of a situation. We mentally step outside an interaction and watch what's happening from a detached perspective. From this place, we can get a different perspective, a helicopter view. It is an extremely useful technique in conflict or when faced with aggressive behaviour. We can disassociate by taking the other person's perspective, often referred to as **position two**, but we shall be talking here about **position three**, from where we can see both position one (ourselves) and position two (the other person).

Sometimes we naturally drift into a disassociated state when we get bored and experience a sort of floating-off feeling. We might drift back into being associated when something happens to bring us back – such as laughter, hearing our name being mentioned or someone nudging us! The gift of being able to deliberately choose to become associated or disassociated enables us to apply an NLP technique to manage our state so we become more resourceful. We would choose to be associated when we want to be fully 'in the moment' and empathize with a friend, support a colleague or enjoy an emotional film. It's the state we use for anchoring because we want to collect the essential intensity of the emotion, to anchor it at the most extreme, so that we can resurrect it whenever we apply the anchor and want to get that intense emotion such as confidence, happiness, success. When we need to focus and concentrate in an exam or for a sport, the only way we can do this is to be associated. Imagine trying to put a key in a keyhole with your mental state floating off somewhere else?!

We want to be disassociated when the going gets tough and we fear we might break down, cry, lose our temper, hit someone or otherwise 'lose the plot'. When we go outside ourselves by disassociating, we ease ourselves out of the intensity, step away from the battlefield and think more clearly about our next move or what we want to say. It gives us the chance to look at the situation more objectively and from another perspective. Sometimes, when we find ourselves getting depressed or overwhelmed with emotion and stress, taking this helicopter view can allow us to be more realistic about our situation. Things are never quite as bad as they seem when we step away. You can learn and observe more easily from a distance and select the parts you want to retain and repeat, rejecting those that are not needed. You aren't completely free of feelings when you are disassociated; you will just not be drowning in them.

THERE AND BACK AGAIN

Here's an exercise to enable you to consciously move yourself from associated to disassociated and back again several times. When you can do this consciously you'll be able to recognize where you are subconsciously and change to where you need to be for the situation you're in. For example, if you find yourself drifting off when you're in the middle of writing, you can ensure that you meet your deadline by quickly associating

- **To associate** – sit quietly and think about something really nice, a happy time, somewhere beautiful or with friends or family. You decide what you want to focus on. When you've got the memory, imagine it's happening right now, today. You are living it as though it's right here in the room. You can hear the people, see the scene and feel what you are feeling.
- **To disassociate** – imagine you have moved out of your own body and you are the other side of the room or above you looking down on someone (you) and watching them enjoy this happy time. Notice everything you see and hear happen to yourself as if you are the observer and not the participant in the action.

What do you notice that's different when you associate and when you disassociate?

DEALING WITH CONFLICT

Disassociation is a great technique for dealing with conflict. Whether this is at work, at home or school, there will be times when disagreements get out of hand. One person gets overexcited, 'loses the plot' and maybe says something out of order that turns a disagreement into a row.

At this point, it is really important for you to be able to disassociate. Even in that split-second heat of the moment, you can quickly step out of yourself and have a quick look to see what's going on.

Imagine for a moment you can zoom up above and look down. Can you step into each person's shoes? Can you see what position one wants and position two? How could you help them to resolve their issue? What needs to happen?

Just the act of stepping out of the situation emotionally takes the heat out of potentially explosive conflict. It also enables you to find points of agreement. Arguments are constant mismatch patterns and this is bad for rapport, unless each person actually prefers to mismatch, in which case you will spot that from the disassociated view. If they don't, or at least one of them doesn't, then they are not in rapport and they need to find points on which to match. Can you see one from the helicopter view?

OVERCOMING NEGATIVE FEELINGS

There are times when we feel low and disheartened. Perhaps we're trying to lose weight and it's hard, or we're studying for an exam and lose motivation, or we're bringing up children and feel we're making a poor job of it. At times like this, it can be easy to fall into such an associated state that we feel overwhelmed. This is a great opportunity to use disassociation. In this instance, position one remains 'you', but position two is your limiting belief about your inability to do something you want to do.

Find somewhere quiet and acknowledge that unresourceful associated feeling. Locate it. Maybe it's in your head or your stomach; it could be in your heart. Imagine what it looks like. Does it have a colour? What size is it? Is there a texture to it? Is it hard or soft? Is it like something else? Give a sense of identity to it. If it could speak or make a sound, what sound would it make and what would it say?

Now this is a tricky one – what does it want for you, what purpose does it have? Can you reassure it that you are OK and don't need it to be there?

The next step is, once you have a good sense of it, to imagine that you could change the colour to one you like and that looks attractive and not off-putting or threatening any more. Change its texture to something furry or more appealing to you. You have the power of your mind to change this into something you can reach in, take hold of and throw away or put on one side.

Now imagine that you could look at yourself from above, as if you were a CCTV camera or a helicopter looking down. What do you see now that you're free of this limiting belief that's dogged you for so long? Do you now see someone resourceful and able to do what you set your mind to? I hope so.

Putting it all together

Disassociation is like an out-of-body experience, giving us the ability to take an objective, dispassionate view of a situation, listen to both sides of an argument, whether the argument is within you or outside you, and take an uninvolved angle on events. Once you have practised it a few times you'll be able to do it 'at the drop of a hat', which is just as well because it does need to be done in an instant in many cases to avert the conflict or depression escalating. Using this NLP technique gives you the opportunity to manage your state.

44 Aim for what you want less of

'NLP believes that you cannot solve a problem with the same thinking that created the problem. By thinking differently you will behave differently and with this combination you can be assured of achieving the results you have been looking for.'
Jeff Archer

 'What the mind can conceive and believe, it can achieve.'
Napoleon Hill

'You must begin to think of yourself as becoming the person you want to be.' David Viscott

'Take care of your body, it's the only place you have to live.'
Jim Rohn

'The difference between Try and Triumph is just a little umph.'
Marvin Phillips

As Christmas approaches and we are bombarded with ads showing festive tables groaning with delicious food, we know that we will pile on some pounds over the festive period. It's the same with holiday times and parties. Afterwards, we promise ourselves that we must lose that extra weight. We are aiming for less weight. This 'wanting less' will also be relevant if you decide to cut down your consumption of alcohol or cigarettes.

In NLP terms, this is an 'away from' goal, but we should be focusing on a 'towards' goal such as aiming for the size we want to be or the weight we would deem desirable. But we don't, do we? We look at the scales and want to see less weight each time we check. Slimming clubs focus on how much weight is lost each week at the weigh-in and this is because that is our focus, too. Of course, we may also be quite particular about where we want to lose the weight from, which is difficult to control.

Another factor is that in order to lose weight we have to eat less and we worry that we may feel hungry and then be tempted to eat the wrong thing because in dieting there are 'right foods' and 'wrong foods', and in general the more tempting they are the more 'wrong' they are. So we need to eat less of these 'wrong' foods, the fattening ones.

Psychologically, all this focus on 'less of' means that we associate dieting with deprivation in a negative way – despite the encouragement to eat more vegetables and drink more water, we tend to focus on the fact that in order to lose weight we need to eat less food and drink less alcohol. Dieting will not be a happy activity when we spend all our time thinking about what we can't eat.

With all this negativity about dieting, we need to have a positive end in sight, to be able to visualize ourselves as we want to be – slim and healthy. If you hold on to the identity of being an overweight person, a smoker or a drinker, that's who you will continue to be. Instead, close your eyes and see yourself as you want to look. Focus on every part of you, how your hair will look, your face, your body and the clothes you'll be wearing. What will you see, hear and feel when you are a slim person? When you keep that picture in your mind, you are well on the way to making it your reality. You need to take on a new identity to get new beliefs and habits. Ask yourself: 'Would I do this if I were a slim person?'

CHANGING YOUR IDENTITY

Changing your identity into a slim person, a non-smoker or a casual drinker means that you have to make changes in other areas of your life in order to align yourself with your goals.

Looking at the Logical Levels diagram in the Appendix, take yourself to the level below identity and think about what **beliefs and values** you have to support your goal. Why is it important for you to take care of your health and to be concerned about how you look and feel? What does losing weight give you that is important to you?

Look at **skills**. What skills and capabilities do you need to lose weight? Where in your life do you have these? You do have them. We have all the resources we need already.

You will need **behaviour** to secure your goal. Different behaviour is needed to lose weight. How will you plan your life to ensure that you do what you need to do?

Your **environment** is where you work, live and the people you interact with daily. They need to support your goal, too, and your fitness and exercise regime. How can you get them on board?

Once you've been down the levels and considered each one, deciding what needs to be done to align them to your new identity, go back up them again to check that they are aligned. Then return to identity and look at your purpose. What will achieving this goal give you in terms of your bigger purpose in life? Perhaps being able to lose weight will mean that you can then tackle other goals with the same approach.

'DON'T!'

The word 'don't' is an embedded command in NLP. When someone says, 'Don't think about pink elephants,' what's the first thing you think about? Pink elephants, of course! You have to, in order to make sense of the instruction. So when we say to ourselves 'Don't eat that cake,' 'Don't have another cigarette' or 'Don't have another drink,' we actually focus on that thing we want, making it much harder to resist.

Instead, make it easier by focusing on what you *do* want. Tell yourself to have something healthier than the cake, something that will help you lose weight and will make you feel good about yourself. When you have the cake you will regret it instantly as all your healthy eating will be wasted and you will have let yourself down. We all know that feeling of temporary happiness followed by a feeling of failure. So when you are just about to tell yourself 'Don't…', stop and think: 'Now what do I want instead?'

'I CAN'T...'

This is an example of a limiting belief. Our beliefs can get in the way of us achieving our goals, so now is the time to jettison those beliefs that are unhelpful regarding losing weight or consuming less of something (it could apply to alcohol or cigarettes or anything you want less of in your life).

Write down all the things you believe about dieting – write a list. Then cross out all those that are unhelpful and look at the beliefs that will be good to focus on. You may want to write those on a sticky note and pop it on your fridge or computer screen.

The beliefs that won't serve a useful purpose may have been relevant in the past; you may have experienced these things but they are going to limit your success so we don't want them now. We can get rid of beliefs very easily by dismissing them in the same way as we don't believe in the tooth fairy anymore. We question the belief and ask it whether we have good grounds, knowledge and experience to believe it now and, if we don't, then we can discard it.

We can also find exceptions to those beliefs. For example, say if one of our beliefs was that losing weight is boring, think about other things you do that are boring – housework, the accounts, weeding, tidying your kids' bedrooms. You do those things and yet they're boring, so what is your belief about those things that you do do? Perhaps you do those boring things because otherwise, if you didn't do them, things would get out of hand and they will look much nicer and neater once they're done. Is that a belief that could help you with your weight-loss goal?

We can find out more about resourceful beliefs by asking people who have successfully lost weight what their beliefs were about it. You can try their beliefs 'on for size' by acting as if you had that belief. You can even 'walk in their shoes' by watching what and how they eat that makes them successful. Perhaps they make different choices at the buffet, eat more slowly, drink more water, have a smaller portion.

The old beliefs were not resourceful in helping you lose weight; you need some different beliefs now.

Question old beliefs that aren't helpful about your ability to do less of something and replace those beliefs with new ones that will enable you to achieve your goal. They may be beliefs you hold in a different area of your life, which you now need to transfer to where you need them, or they may be someone else's, which you can adopt as your own. Focus on what you can do and want to do, rather than what you can't or don't want to do, and visualize yourself as the slim, healthy person you aspire to be. Align yourself to your goals and get everyone around you on board, supporting you.

45 Assess the importance of other people's opinions

'Team leaders can motivate the people in their teams especially well when they understand the referencing that each member of the team uses. It becomes a great deal easier to create meaningful feelings for the members of a team when you know what matters to them.' David Ferrers

'The best style is to have an internal reference with an external check. That is, we use our own values, beliefs, visions; outcomes, etc. as our stabilizing gyroscope and regularly look outside of ourselves to see how it fits with the world of others and the state of knowledge. We then feel centred in ourselves, in our values, standards, beliefs, understandings, visions, goals, etc. and then fully open and responsive to information and perceptions outside of ourselves.' Steve Jabba

'How sensitive you are to other people's opinions and feedback determines how much you are affected by the achievement culture.' Joseph O'Connor

'Have you ever noticed a person who, when making a suggestion in a meeting, glances in the direction of someone from whom they are seeking approval? It may not be the person to whom they are making the suggestion but it is the person whose feedback and acknowledgment they rely on for feedback on how they are doing.' Sue Knight

'To identify whether your children are internal or external ask them a question such as "At school, how do you know

you've written a good essay?" An internal child may say, "I just know or it feels right." An external child may say, "My teacher needs to give me a good mark, say nice things or smile at me."' Roger Ellerton

We seem to be in an age where other people's opinions almost garner more importance than our own as we seek out Facebook 'Likes', 'Follows' on Twitter and other social media, and a huge list of contacts on our mobile phone. As soon as there is a decision to make, we can be sharing it with friends and 'googling' options. This is called being 'externally referenced' and it is one option, the other being 'internally referenced'. They both lie on a continuum and it is for you to decide where you want to operate depending on the situation or decision in hand.

Being internally referenced means that we go inside ourselves to interpret how we feel, what we want to do, how to respond or decide. An externally referenced person would, instead, ask someone else for advice (if they were auditory), notice other people's reactions (if they were visual) and sense their reactions (if they were kinaesthetic). This is on a sliding scale rather than being bipolar. In some situations we might look to others for a response whereas in other situations, perhaps when and where we feel more confident, we would rely on our own judgement and decision-making ability. If, however, you find yourself regularly at one end of the scale or the other, it might be refreshing to consider being more flexible.

We make decisions based on our interpretation of a situation. As something happens, we filter it in various ways. We may delete parts of what happened based on whether we tend to focus on what we see, hear or feel. We also tend to respond according to the language that is used. Perhaps the way something is communicated really annoys you or the tone sounds offensive or it is said so quickly that you can't quite follow it or so quietly that you struggle to hear it.

Communication also gets distorted when we assume intentions that may not be there, so that we are almost mind-reading the situation. Then we might generalize, telling ourselves that this *'always* happens' or that *'no one ever* takes any notice of what we say'. The next filter that comes into play is that we set the event against our values and beliefs about what is important to us, what is right and what is wrong. These come from our upbringing and experiences in life; the latter may constantly change but our core values tend to remain constant. Around most subjects we have acquired attitudes from reading and discussions that have built a fund of knowledge which we can apply to the event that has occurred. Again, our attitudes are constantly changing as we meet new people and learn new things, and this event is part of the learning process.

Past experiences and memories also play a part in forming our response to this event as we recall what happened in the past and whether we want to repeat the process this time or do something different.

People who are internally referenced go through these processes to interpret events and then, on the basis of the internal processing, respond with little regard for the opinions of others. This can result in a rather abrupt, even rude response that might even be hurtful, although those who are internally referenced won't be so concerned about that aspect. When you are externally referenced little processing takes place; instead, other people's opinions are sought through various means such as posting on social media, texting, asking immediately 'What do you think?' or waiting to see what others do and acting accordingly. While in some situations this latter approach may be workable, it doesn't encourage any independent thought or feeling, and this means that you may be unprepared for situations when this is required.

IMAGINE YOURSELF IN SOMEONE ELSE'S SHOES

If you find yourself at the internal referencing end of the scale, before you say or do anything you need to second-position it. This means putting yourself into the shoes of the other person. You may like to practise this now, so you find it easy to do when you need to.

Think of a situation that occurred recently, a conversation perhaps. Recall what was said and imagine you are the other person, the person you were talking to.

- What were they thinking about what you said?
- Did they agree with you?

- Could you have expressed yourself in a way they would have preferred or found easier to understand?
- Are they visual, auditory or kinaesthetic? Could you have had more rapport if you'd matched their language?
- What would have happened if you'd asked their opinion?
- Did you think about their feelings when you did what you did or said what you said?

Now run through the situation again, making a point of bearing in mind that what you say and do affects the other person and that they can have an input that will increase rapport and could improve the final result.

JUST STOP

If you think you may be rather too externally referenced, try this:

STOP

Yes, add a gap before responding to anything. Instead of instantly texting a friend or retweeting something, ask yourself 'What do I think about this?' It's not enough to simply 'like' something or agree with it. Run through it again and think about what was said or done.

- Does it accord with your own values and beliefs?
- Is it 'the right thing to do'?
- Will anyone else be hurt/offended and does this matter to you?
- Do you agree with the views expressed?
- Would you prefer to opt out or add something to what has been said?

Think about the information going through the filters and check whether you feel completely in alignment about it. When something doesn't feel quite right, we may feel uncomfortable and sometimes we even hold ourselves slightly off centre as our body reflects the incongruence we feel.

Imagine you are someone uninvolved in the situation, an innocent bystander, a CCTV camera, a fly on the wall. What would you think about what you are witnessing?

It's easy in today's fast-paced environment, with technology that can communicate our words at a fraction of a second all over the world, for us to say something that someone else would be offended or upset by. Rather than risk this, think about the filters. You are responsible for the communications you make; it is not for the other person to have to guess what you meant. Make sure you feel comfortable about how you communicate. The communication has to sit comfortably with you and be in alignment with your own identity, values and beliefs.

LET OTHERS MAKE UP THEIR MINDS

As a parent we forget, however old our children are, that they have an opinion. Even parents of grown-up children with children of their own can sometimes internally reference when communicating with them because this is what they're used to. This is sometimes how young people get to be so externally referenced because no one has ever encouraged them to make their own mind up.

When our parents were children themselves, they had much more freedom from parental control and had to take responsibility for themselves in a way their own children can't. If you have to get yourself to school and are used to playing in the street or unsupervised, you're going to be much more aware of the implications of your actions.

However old you are, when communicating with others it is not OK to do the thinking for them. Instead, work on building rapport and mutual respect by eliciting their opinions, expressing your own and being willing to sit in the middle of the internally/externally referenced scale where you learn from others and can be flexible and responsible.

Putting it all together

Being completely internally or externally referenced is unworkable in social interactions. Although we need to take into consideration other people's feelings and how what we say and do affects them, we also need to stay true to our own values and beliefs while being prepared to increase our knowledge and change our attitudes when new information challenges long-held beliefs. Remember, you once believed in Father Christmas. Beliefs change.

46 Time-travel your way to confidence

'Man often becomes what he believes himself to be. If I keep on saying to myself that I cannot do a certain thing, it is possible that I may end by really becoming incapable of doing it. On the contrary, if I have the belief that I can do it, I shall surely acquire the capacity to do it even if I may not have it at the beginning.' Mahatma Gandhi

'A dame that knows the ropes isn't likely to get tied up.' Mae West

'When I was a child my mother said to me, "If you become a soldier, you'll be a general. If you become a monk, you'll be the pope." Instead I became a painter and wound up as Picasso.'
Pablo Picasso

'Somehow I can't believe that there are any heights that can't be scaled by a man who knows the secrets of making dreams come true. This special secret, it seems to me, can be summarized in four Cs. They are curiosity, confidence, courage, and constancy, and the greatest of all is confidence. When you believe in a thing, believe in it all the way, implicitly and unquestionably.' Walt Disney

'Believe in yourself! Have faith in your abilities! Without a humble but reasonable confidence in your own powers you cannot be successful or happy.' Norman Vincent Peale

At various stages in our life, we experience crises of confidence, sometimes at quite unexpected moments when it can be embarrassing or inconvenient. Lack of confidence also often descends on us after a major life-changing event such as divorce or bereavement, moving home, a change of job or having a baby. How great would it be to be able to feel confident whenever you need to.

When you are not feeling confident, you may think that this is a familiar state and worry that you are not a confident person. When we do this, we are making our state of mind dictate our identity, which is not a fair reflection. A 'not confident' state is a temporary feeling brought about by fear of the unknown or fear of repeating a bad experience from the past. We can manage this by revisiting the experience and reliving it, using an NLP technique called **timeline**.

We make sense of external events, things that we experience, in a unique way based on our own personal past, the way we've been brought up, our values and beliefs and the way we have managed those situations before. Filters come into play that distort, generalize and delete information from these experiences, resulting in us having our own perception of it. We might, for example, generalize by saying that we 'never have any confidence in social situations' or that 'we always freeze when we are introduced to new people'. An example of distortion is when we suggest someone else has 'made us' lack confidence or that 'travelling by air makes us scared', rather than taking responsibility for our own state. Deletion is when we omit to take into account the whole picture or experience and just extract the bit that 'proves' our point.

By using the timeline and revisiting past experiences we have the opportunity to look at them again with hindsight and with an older mind. We can use it to re-examine what happened, albeit our own perception of it, in a controlled situation where we can look at the whole picture, not just the snapshot that has formed our perception. We have the opportunity to remove the generalizations, distortions and deletions and relive it.

We will also use the timeline to find occasions in our life when we were confident and resourceful. By anchoring that state, we can then bring it to where we need it today.

WALKING THE TIMELINE

Imagine a line on the floor in front of you. One end of it is when you were a small child and the other end is old age. Place yourself on it at a point that reflects approximately the stage you are at today.

Now think about how you are feeling now, about the lack of confidence you're experiencing and the situation in which it presents itself. Associate into it by really experiencing it as if it's happening right now: see what you see, hear what's going on around you as you feel lacking in confidence, and feel the emotions and do the actions using your body to express what's going on for you now.

You're going to be anchoring confidence in a minute, so you need an action that you will be able to link to that feeling. Most people use a squeeze of the earlobe or they make a 'thumbs-up' sign or put their thumb and first finger together to make a circle. Decide what yours will be, practise it a few times. Make sure it's something you'll be able to do discreetly.

Now look back along the timeline and go and stand at the point when you feel you were confident about this situation or a similar situation. Imagine you are experiencing it with confidence right now. Again, associate into it, seeing what is around you, hearing what is being said and doing whatever you are doing. Imagine it like a film in which you are playing the lead role. Give it colour and volume – really live it! When it seems very real to you, use your anchor. Hold it and keep experiencing that wonderful confident feeling – it's happening *now*. As it starts to fade, remove your anchor and give yourself a little shake. You have anchored a confident state, and whenever you need to feel confident you can use this action to remind yourself of this confident time.

To make the anchor work really well, repeat the action a few times as you relive the experience.

BACK TO THE FUTURE

We can also travel in the other direction along the timeline. Maybe you can't think of a time in the past when you've ever felt confident. In that case, go and stand on the timeline in the future at the point when you *will* feel confident.

At that point, associate into the confident feeling and anchor it. It's great that you can imagine being confident. Look up and to the right to visualize how confident you will be and put yourself in the situation where you are confident, as if it's happening today.

Once you've done that, start walking back to today's point with your anchor in place and experience that lovely confident feeling. If at any point you feel it diminishing, it could be that you are worrying about some upcoming event, so disassociate for a moment by hovering above the timeline so you can look at the event more dispassionately. Be curious about what there is about it that you can't handle confidently with your anchor in place.

USE THE TIMELINE TO DISASSOCIATE

We can use the timeline in another way. Having anchored our confidence, we can walk it back to today's point on the timeline.

Anchor the confidence again at the point where you were on the timeline for the last exercise. Now take one step towards today's place. Stop after one step. Is the confidence still there? If it is, walk another step; if it isn't, stop.

If you've had to stop altogether, you can do a disassociating exercise. Remember how, in order to anchor, we associated? We want to separate ourselves now and disassociate in order to find out what has happened to our confident feeling, as it seems to have disappeared momentarily.

Imagine you can hover above the timeline like a CCTV camera looking down on yourself. What do you see? Can you understand what has happened to affect that confident feeling? Maybe something significant has happened in your life to reduce your confidence. When you know what it is, come back down to the line again and use your confidence anchor to feel confident again. Take another step.

Continue walking towards today's point on the line, pausing to hover above the line and disassociate when you need to. Aim to be standing back at today's point on the line, full of confidence.

Putting it all together

Using the timeline is an excellent way to explore how past confidence and future possibilities of confidence can be harnessed, anchored and brought into your skill set for use today and for whenever you need them. The timeline can be used for a number of purposes and different skills, so once you've used it for confidence you could have a go at finding other resources that you need and time-travel in just the same way as has been described here. So long as you have ever had the skill or could imagine having it, then the timeline is a great tool. Help others to recover mislaid skills with this technique or encourage them to visualize having a skill they need in the future.

47

Remember the time when you didn't have that fear

> 'The Law of Dominant Thought says that what you focus on increases so the more we think about failure or not performing well, the more it is likely to happen.' Jeremy Lazarus

> 'Babies are born with only two fears: the fear of falling and the fear of loud noises. All other human fears are learned. Therefore, if you learned to be afraid, you can learn to be unafraid.' Richard Bandler

> 'Fear is that little darkroom where negatives are developed.' Michael Pritchard

> 'The feeling comes from a process in the body that is triggered by something we see, hear, feel, touch, taste or smell. And these sights, sounds and feelings can arise from the outside world or from our imagination. Whatever the origin, fear is not something we have, but something we do.' Joseph O'Connor

> 'For many individuals, it's simply the anticipated anxiety they'd experience if they were unable to turn their dreams into reality that prevents them from taking the first steps.' Jeff Archer

The fear that you have now hasn't always been with you, although sometimes it may seem like that because you have had to develop coping strategies that have become part of your life. The fact that there has been life without the fear means that you will be free of it again because you have the memory of not having had it.

There are two elements of fear. The first is the **trigger**, the actual event, and the second is the **meaning** we make of it. We each have a different map of the world based on our memories and experiences, beliefs and values, so you will have fears that are unique to you both in terms of content and severity. What all our fears have in common is that underlying them is a fear of losing something we value: our health, life itself, our self-esteem or our wellbeing. Using NLP, we can focus on the meaning our brain makes of the trigger and train it to make a different meaning of it.

This is much easier than you might imagine. Do you remember when losing a tooth meant that the tooth fairy would visit and leave you a coin under your pillow? Well, it's doubtful whether this is still the meaning you give to losing a tooth! The belief you have about something changes and, while you did believe once that the tooth fairy would visit, you don't now. Similarly, you need to change the belief underpinning your fear, because, once, you didn't hold that belief, so it's important to consider what has changed. The factor that changes our belief is knowledge and experience. Once you've seen your mum sneak a coin under your pillow in the night, you know that either a) she is the tooth fairy or b) there isn't a tooth fairy. It's the same with fear. When you increase your knowledge, you will hold a different belief about the thing that you fear, one that will diminish it.

Your current fear has a positive intention. Maybe you fear something now because you are less agile, more cautious, older. For example, it is probably quite sensible for someone in their 50s who hasn't skied for many years to fear going down an icy black slope, even though in their youth they weren't afraid to do so. In this case, your present fear is keeping you safe. You can rid yourself of the fear by learning how to ski that type of slope, practising on gentler ones and preparing your body for skiing. What is the positive intention of your fear? When you know what it is, you can think about how you could satisfy this positive intention without having the fear response. But fear is illogical, and even though you haven't always had this fear, you have it now and no amount of rationalizing, knowledge or avoidance will make it go away – so what do you do?

In the following boxes are some great NLP techniques for getting rid of fear. Try them.

ANCHORING

At the moment, we have an unhelpful unconscious anchor (the trigger) that creates a meaning and a fear response that we don't want. Instead, we can replace this unconscious anchor (which might be the sight, sound or touch of something) with a conscious anchor to create a new meaning and a new resourceful response, which will be a calm state.

To anchor, find somewhere quiet and decide what action you want to use as your anchor. Most people use a squeeze of the earlobe, a 'thumbs-up' sign or they touch their thumb and first finger together to form a circle or 'OK' sign. Practise this a few times so that you can use it without having to think about it.

Now think about the response you'd like to make to the event that usually scares you, your trigger. You haven't always had this fear, so you may want to concentrate your mind on how you used to respond to this trigger. Imagine that you are feeling that feeling now (the one you want) – see what you see and hear what you hear. When the feeling is very strong, use your anchor and keep it there until the sensations pass.

Repeat this a few times but take breaks in between by shaking yourself or walking around a bit because it is quite an intense sensation and the anchor will be more effective if, when you repeat it, you do it from the starting point of being relaxed.

Now use this anchor when you encounter your trigger and you will have a conscious anchor to replace the unconscious one.

REFRAME FAILURE AS FEEDBACK

For many people, fear of failure is a fear they experience as they get older and didn't have as a child. This is because the stakes are higher and what you may be required to do is more complex and potentially scarier.

It can be helpful to reframe failure as feedback. Imagine if you believed that all failure was feedback. Remember that fear has a positive intention. It can be there to give you feedback. This could be feedback about potential danger, or it could be feedback that you can learn from in order to perform better. When we experience fear, it gives us heightened awareness and this can help us give a better performance, whether that is in sport, on the stage or socially. If we didn't care and were totally relaxed, this wouldn't be the best state for a good result.

Instead of focusing on what you can't do or may not be able to do, think about what you can do and the skills you have. We already have all the resources we need, so somewhere in your life you have the skills to succeed in what you want to achieve. Find them and remind yourself that these skills will ensure your success. You also have the skill to learn what you currently don't know, so add new skills and you can achieve whatever you set out to do.

USE A TIMELINE TO LOSE YOUR FEAR

We are going to use a timeline to explore how to be free of this fear.

Imagine a line on the floor at one end of which is your childhood and at the other end old age. We don't need to be precise about dates or ages but simply establish the points that represent present, past and future time.

Stand on the point that is today and think about that fear, how you feel when you are in the situation of which you are fearful, and imagine yourself there right now. What can you see, hear and feel? As you imagine it happening now, turn up the sound and colour to make it vibrant and notice who else is there, what they are doing, saying and how you are reacting. Notice your physiology at this point.

When you've had enough of that, shake yourself off and come off the timeline for a moment.

Now, when you are ready, find a point on the timeline in the past when you didn't have that fear. Stand on that point and think about the same situation that you experienced just now, but without the fear. What do you notice?

You can notice more when you disassociate. To do this, imagine floating up above your timeline and looking down on yourself at that age and point in your life. What do you see? Is there anything you notice from this position that you didn't notice from first position when you were associated?

Sometimes, when we do this, we understand how we came to have our fear and realize that we can choose not to have it anymore.

Stay in this time when you had no fear and walk slowly back to today's point on the timeline. If at any point you start to experience a sense of fear, hover above again and decide whether you want that fear or not. Using the timeline shows you that your response is a choice. You didn't always make this choice and you don't have to make it now. You can choose not to have this fear.

Putting it all together

Almost all fears are acquired through copying our parents or from negative experiences we have had that have taught us that this thing is to be feared. However, we can relearn through increased knowledge about it, acquiring anchoring skills and by going back in time to when we did not have this response and reframing it.

48 SWISH away those bedtime monsters

'There are few monsters who warrant the fear we have of them.' André Gide

'Courage is resistance to fear, mastery of fear, not absence of fear.' Mark Twain

'People sometimes think that because children fear things that are strange or unreasonable (at least to our adult reason) their fears are less intense and less important. But fear is based on perception, not reality. It is worse for children if adults ridicule their fears. They have to cope with the fear and the ridicule.' Joseph O'Connor

'The most important thing to remember is that for children, fears are very real, just as they are for adults. The process of normalizing fears begins with acknowledging them, listening carefully and then working with the child to reframe the fear into an articulated, manageable scenario.' Jennifer Syrkiewicz

'Nothing in life is to be feared, it is only to be understood. Now is the time to understand more so that we may fear less.' Marie Curie

It's not unusual for children to have disturbing dreams about monsters and dragons, witches and aliens. Sometimes these occur at night-time but sometimes it can be as they are going to bed and feeling drowsy. It can be disturbing for parents and siblings, so how can we use NLP to get rid of them for ever?

Children have a fantastic imagination. They aren't constrained by what is possible as we are and they can easily morph things they've seen in a book into living, breathing creatures in their room. The most important thing is to acknowledge the fear. However tired you are or however many times your child has done this, you should still accept that for them there really are monsters under the bed, in the wardrobe, behind the door or wherever they are. Suggesting that they are imagining them just makes them feel stupid and this isn't helpful long term. Telling them not to cry or be a baby also doesn't help because they are not doing this intentionally. It may also predispose them to keep other fears to themselves when they get older.

Your child will need a coping strategy because you won't always be around when they have these fears. They could occur when they are at a sleepover or away at camp, or while staying with grandparents or family friends. Although now the fear may be monsters, later on in life your child may fear other things, so having a strategy to overcome fear will be a resourceful skill to have – whether it is monsters now or exams later on.

ZAP THAT MONSTER

The first thing is to find the **trigger**. What happens just before the monster appears? We're not talking here about the trigger that might be what is prompting them to feel a bit sensitive in the first place but what prompted the fear response that is their worry now. Was it when you turned the light off or did their dressing gown look like a monster? Did they think they saw something under the bed? Let's call that 'the trigger'.

Ask them what they'd like to see instead of the monster. Ask them to imagine something nice they'd like to see or hear. Can they picture what they'd like to see instead? Get them to draw a picture of it or describe it to you and give it a name. Perhaps it could be you they'd like to see instead, or their favourite TV character or teddy bear? Once they've decided what it is they'd like instead, give them an imaginary zapper or remote control, magic wand (use whatever word will suit the situation and their age and imagination) and say, 'Now when you next see your monster, I want you to point your remote control at it and press it so you change the picture to the one you want to see. When you press it I want you to say SWISH and then the monster will change into what you have decided you want instead.' You can practise this a few times with them. If they have the imagination to see monsters, they can certainly press an imaginary remote control and change the monster into a superhero or favourite toy or animal.

USE SUBMODALITIES

Because children have such great imaginations, we can use this to morph the monsters into less scary creatures and get rid of them altogether. How we do that is by getting them to describe what they see, the monster they experience now.

If they describe it in visual terms using colour, size and appearance, maybe the shape of their eyes and ears, ask them:

- Can you change its colour? What colour would you like it to be?
- Can you make it smaller?
- Can you give it a smiley face?
- Can you make it wear spotty pyjamas?
- Can you give it a sunhat?
- Can you give it some furry slippers with a bunny on the front?

The thing is to remember that this is an imaginary monster, so children can use the power of their imagination to turn it into something funny or less scary.

If they describe it in auditory terms – maybe it's noisy or making a horrible sound – then ask them to imagine they have a volume switch and they can turn down the volume or make it into a nice sound:

- Can you turn down the volume?
- Can you ask your monster to sing a nursery rhyme?
- Can your monster whisper?

If your child is kinaesthetic and is talking about what the monster is doing, ask him to tell it to stop:

- Can you ask your monster to do what he's doing but in the garden?

- Can your monster go away?
- Can your monster tidy your bedroom instead of keeping you awake?

What we're doing is acknowledging that they do have a monster in their imagination but, because it is in their imagination and does not exist and is not in your imagination, they have the power to change it. Introducing children at an early age to the power they have to control how they think and create more resourceful thoughts is, as you can imagine, an extremely useful skill in life.

WHAT IS THE MONSTER LIKE?

If your child is quite **visual**, ask them to draw their monster. Encourage them to use coloured pencils and let them draw all the detail. This will work even if your child seems too young to draw; it still gives an outlet for their imagination.

If your child is **auditory** and likes talking, ask them to describe their monster. What does their monster look like, sound like, what does he do and does he talk to them?

With a **kinaesthetic** child who is more action-oriented, ask what their monster likes to do, what he is doing now, where has he been, how does he feel. Is he warm enough?

Be curious. Not only do these talks help dispel their fears of the monster directly but they also give you an opportunity to pick up on any other fears that they may have. As children start to describe their monster, it becomes less scary and the fact that they can see that you aren't scared by it will reassure them.

Giving the monster a name helps, too; after all, how scary can a monster be when it has a name? A very imaginative child may let you talk to their monster, in which case you can ask it very sweetly to go back home and let your child get some sleep.

Be clear, though, that this monster is in the child's imagination, even though it seems very real to them. You could tell your child that lots of children have these fears and imaginary monsters. Perhaps you did when you were young.

Putting it all together

Preschool children often have monster dreams and can wake up scared at night. Some older children can go through anxious periods when they do the same. Acknowledge that their fear is real but that the monsters are in their imagination, because otherwise they'd see them out and about in the supermarket or at school. Establishing a calm and consistent bedtime routine helps keep children reassured, as does making sure they don't watch scary programmes or read scary books before going to bed. Leave the door slightly open and a light on. If they still have a 'monster moment', talk to them about their monster and use the SWISH technique or submodalities to get rid of it.

49

Be the best presenter in your team

❝ '*If you're presenting yourself with confidence, you can pull off pretty much anything.*' Katy Perry

❝ '*The only way to feel more comfortable about speaking in public is to do it well and more often. As you build up memories of positive experiences, of trying new things, you'll quickly start feeling (and looking) relaxed and capable when you speak to groups of people.*' Harry Key

❝ '*The best way to persuade someone is not through rational facts and information, but through convincing narration or dramatic storytelling.*' Walter Fisher

❝ '**Do it more.** *Take as many opportunities as you can to speak, with as little time in between as possible. As your body gets used to the experience of standing up in front of crowds, your stress hormone levels will normalise, and you'll start to feel more relaxed. Focus on letting yourself be yourself. It'll feel more familiar and give you access to your sense of humour, making you more friendly and relatable.*

'**Do it differently.** *Try doing your presentation a bunch of different ways, particularly if you're giving the same talk over and over again. It'll keep things alive in your mind, and it will give you a richer arsenal of experiences to draw upon.*' Harry Key

❝ '*No one can remember more than three points.*' Philip Crosby

Wherever you work, you will at some point be expected to present something. It could be a short explanation about something you're working on to the rest of your team or your manager, or you might have to present on a bigger scale at a conference or board meeting. For some people, even presenting to a smaller group can be a terrifying prospect, let alone presenting to a large room full of people. However, the skills are the same.

One of the fastest ways to change your state is to change your physiology – remember, mind and body are one. How you are feeling is reflected in how you stand, the angle of your head, where you are looking and what you are doing with your hands. So stand straight with your legs slightly apart so your weight is evenly distributed. Hold your hands still and make sure your head is in the middle of your shoulders, with your eyes looking directly ahead. There's no need to glare, but keep making eye contact with people around you. Smile to show you are feeling confident and you will find you actually are!

Set your goal before you even start preparing your presentation. What do you want your audience to come away with? These need to be positive thoughts!

- Why are you speaking? What do you have to say? It's not enough just to want to 'inform people'; this is not active enough.
- Have a well-formed outcome. What do you want them to know and understand? You may have a large amount of data and they won't be able to take in all of it, so what are the key points?
- How are you going to grab their attention to start with?
- What do you want them to feel? What will success look, sound and feel like for you? Decide what feelings you'd like to have expressed as a result. What would your desired feedback be?
- What do you want them to do? What is your call to action? Do you want them to read the longer document, make a decision, ask questions? You need to think about what actions should result from your presentation.

Ask your colleagues for feedback. What do they feel you do well, what could be better and overall what do they think of how you present? Focus on the things they say you do well – how could you make more of this?

People love stories; they don't love facts. Make your points by telling stories to inspire them; make them change an opinion; make them feel strongly about something. You won't do this with PowerPoint slides. If you can **tell** them, do so.

CONCENTRATE ON YOUR BREATHING

When we feel nervous, our breathing seems to come from high up in the throat area. This makes our voice a bit squeaky and it can easily break up, which then makes us feel embarrassed, which impairs our performance even more. So, focus on how you are breathing.

First, drop those tense shoulders. Then breathe in and, as you do so, let your diaphragm fill with air. This will make your belly swell out, so to check that you're doing it correctly gently lay your hands on it and enjoy the feeling as it fills. That oxygen is going to enrich your blood and get those brain cells working.

Now breathe out and encourage all the air out by pressing lightly on your belly, almost squeezing it out. You may even want to blow that last bit out to make sure all that stale air is ejected. Then repeat this breathing and you will notice when you speak that your voice becomes slower and lower. This makes it easier for people to hear you, and the lower voice tone sounds more sincere and believable. It sounds as if you are speaking from a place of conviction.

MODEL THE BEST

You know whose presentations you want to model. Who do you think does a great job? It could be someone in your organization, someone on TV or someone you've watched on YouTube. Take the time before you present to study the style of someone you admire.

Watch them again and again. Copy how they stand, how they hold themselves, how they use gestures. As they do it, you do it too, mimicking them. Exaggerate the movements because when you are actually on stage you will tone them down naturally anyway. Note eye movements. How often do they look up and how do they use eye contact? Is it to emphasize an important point, or is it at the end of sentences? How do they use their eyes? Do they look up occasionally, and which way – right or left? When do they look down?

Listen to their voice; pace it for yourself, noting the pauses. Copy the tone – is it higher or lower than yours? Match the tone and notice what difference it makes.

How do they look? Your audience will make decisions about you from the moment they see you. How does your model presenter look? Make sure you dress appropriately for the audience and for what they expect of you.

Now for the all-important part. How your model presenter acts will be driven by their beliefs about the presentation they are giving. Put yourself into their shoes. What are they thinking? What is important to them? What do they believe about why they are giving the presentation? If your model works with you or you know them, you can find out more by asking them about their beliefs. However, if you don't, you will have to read about them in books, articles and interviews.

FUTURE PACING

Future pacing is a great way to handle presentations. You will need to practise your presentation to check for pace and length, how fast you need to speak and where you need to pause, otherwise you could end up finishing too early or overrunning. This could result in someone senior having to leave before the end and not getting the full benefit of your hard work.

When you are running through your presentation before the event, imagine that this is the actual event and think about how people might be reacting. Visualize what you want to be seeing – people looking at you with interest, paying attention to you, nodding in agreement. Think about what you want to hear – people asking good questions that will enable you to interact fully with the audience and the material, lots of 'yeses' as they agree with what you're saying and a hearty round of applause at the end. Think about what will be happening and how the audience will be feeling — energized, interested, passionate.

If there are places where you want them to laugh, then imagine laughter; and if there are places where they need to be examining data, imagine them focused on it.

Future pacing is about running the presentation through as you want it to be, with excellence.

Putting it all together

You can be the best presenter in your team when you model the best. Practise and 'future pace' your performance and remember to focus on your breathing. Have a clear idea of your outcome and take advantage of feedback.

50 Escape the Drama Triangle

'Participating in the drama of the triangle keeps people stuck in lies, blame and shame, unhealthy secrets, "should" and addictions to crisis, chaos and manipulation.' Lynne Namka

'Our primary positions are generally set up in childhood. For instance, if a parent is overly protective, doing everything for a child, then that child may grow up to feel incapable of taking care of themselves. This sets them up for a lifetime role of victim. Or the opposite, they might come to feel angry and vindictive if others don't take care of them, thereby adopting a primary persecutor stance.' Lynn Forrest

'The secret of being wise is knowing what to pay attention to.' William James

'Yesterday's victims are tomorrow's persecutors.' Victor Schoelcher

'The Karpman Triangle game inhibits real problem solving, creates confusion and distress, not solutions.' Randi Kreger

We're all familiar with fairy stories, aren't we? Which is your favourite? Do you like 'Cinderella and the Ugly Sisters' or 'Red Riding Hood', 'Rapunzel' or 'Snow White'? What they all have in common is that there is a victim, a 'baddie' and a knight in shining armour. In 'Cinderella', the eponymous heroine is the downtrodden victim, the Ugly Sisters are the baddies and the Fairy Godmother, the 'knight in shining armour' (as is the Prince, of course). While we are familiar with these terms in everyday life, Stephen Karpman introduced us to the **Drama Triangle** in 1968 and named the three positions or roles V = Victim, P = Persecutor and R = Rescuer. Intrinsic to the concept is that these are roles that are dynamic and change constantly. The only way to stop the dynamic is to step away from the triangle and take responsibility for oneself.

The **victim** is the one who feels powerless and hopeless, but they can't take that role unless there's a persecutor. The victim feels sorry for themselves and doesn't take responsibility for their feelings. They blame the persecutor, of course, because they avoid confrontation and believe that their needs don't matter. The victim says things like 'Poor me!' The victim has a tendency to be passive-aggressive, to not make decisions or, if they make one, not stick to it. It isn't their fault but the fault of the persecutor, who 'makes them' feel inadequate, and the rescuer, who is always there to help them.

The **rescuer** role is played by someone who, on the face of it, wants to help and be useful. They do things for others as this makes them feel good and it gives them a sense of self-worth. It is therefore in their interests to keep the others dependent on them. 'I'm only trying to help you,' they would say. They will take the moral high ground and be judgemental and take control of situations in order to feel important. There's nothing they like more than for people to be reliant on them. They will then complain that they are being taken advantage of and will typically move into victim position. This role sometimes draws in mothers who feel guilty and the rescuer role fulfils their need to be punished by being a martyr.

The **persecutor** enjoys confrontation and putting others down with their false sense of superiority. They like to be in control and use verbal or physical power to do so. They blame and criticize, and believe they are always right. They will not accept any argument. They are used to getting their own way and feel they have the right to. These negative behaviours cover up their own sense of inadequacy and problems which they dare not face.

Common triangular situations that we experience are teachers/parents/child, father/mother/child, colleague/me/

manager or, more generally, drawback or illness/me/rest of the world. The triangular situation turns bad when someone is not OK about it.

None of these positions is pleasant. Each carries its own kind of pain and discomfort, sense of shame and guilt, loss of personal power and responsibility. Crucially, these roles can be established early on in childhood and can show themselves through adult life, even passing on to the next generation. We move from one to another round the triangle, denying our own feelings and those of others. Each person in the triangle has a primary role but can shift to another when it suits them or when someone else takes their role. Playing the roles always creates lose-lose-lose. No one wins in the Drama Triangle.

HOW DO WE AVOID THE DRAMA TRIANGLE IN THE FIRST PLACE?

Now you know what the three roles are, you will be able to recognize when you find yourself taking one of them.

Don't be a victim. Take care of your own problems rather than expecting someone else to rescue you, unless you expressly ask or seek out advice. Asking for information and advice is an adult–adult transaction and not the action of a victim. Next time you catch yourself thinking 'It's not fair' or 'Why me?', think about how you could do something different to change this outcome for next time.

Don't rescue. Equally, do not offer advice, attempt to help someone who doesn't need your help and in particular step in when it's all about you rather than a genuine desire to help. Asking someone whether they'd like your help is adult–adult and is not rescuing. You are ultimately helping them more by letting them take responsibility for themselves.

Don't persecute. It is not acceptable to blame other people for your situation; instead, figure out a way to solve your problem, ask for help from whomever you need, and however much people might annoy you, just walk away. Whatever has happened is your responsibility and you can sort it out yourself without blaming others.

STEPPING OUT OF THE DRAMA TRIANGLE

If you find yourself already in a Drama Triangle, you've taken the first step in getting out of it! Awareness is that first step. Feel that discomfort and recognize that the situation is not being resolved. Experience the different roles: where are you now and who is taking which role?

Second, separate yourself emotionally by disassociating, which is to float out of your body and view the situation from a distance as if you were a CCTV camera. When you do this, you can more clearly understand and appreciate the dynamics. We observe the triangle from the meta-position.

Thirdly, think about what the positive intention might be for each person in the triangle. We must assume there is one, even if it may be a struggle to find it. What are they getting out of taking this role at this time? Put yourself into their shoes. If you were doing or saying this, what might have prompted it and what could you be hoping for?

Now tell each person what you observe about the situation. It is important not to talk about the person themselves or the role, but just talk about what you can see and hear happening. Find areas of agreement and common intention. Suggest ways in which individual positive intentions of the interaction can be met such that everyone's positive intention is met.

THE INTERNAL DRAMA TRIANGLE

Not only do these triangles exist in our everyday lives at work, school and home, but they also exist inside our own head.

Maybe we are cross with ourselves for having that extra glass of wine and getting silly or argumentative with a friend as a result, missing the train and being late for a date, forgetting to call a new client or a friend's birthday. We are in persecutor role: 'You're useless' we say to ourselves.

We move into victim role and feel bad, angry, disappointed in ourselves: 'I'm so useless' we think.

But then what happens next? We rescue ourselves by saying, 'Well, you were so busy' or 'You hadn't eaten so it went to your head, didn't it?' or 'You shouldn't do so much – take it easy.' We may then have some chocolate or a cigarette because it's been a hard day.

When you find yourself in this internal Drama Triangle, you need to deal with it in just the same way as the external one. Stop. Become aware. Disassociate. Extract the positive intention and find another way to satisfy it by looking at your options. Take responsibility for your behaviour.

Putting it all together

The Drama Triangle plays out in everyday life wherever you work and whomever you socialize with. It even plays out in our head. The thing to recognize is that these are roles, not facts, and they can be changed. You are a part of it and can take responsibility for stopping the game when you distance yourself and notice what's going on. Understand the motive behind each role and what each one wants – their positive intention – then initiate a discussion that will enable their positive intentions to be met by them taking responsibility individually rather than blaming others, being blamed or rescuing.

APPENDIX

The Logical Levels

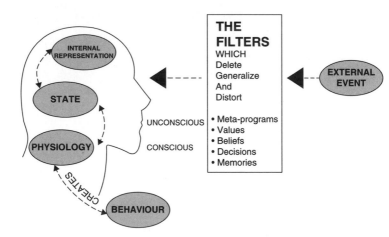

The NLP Communication Model

BIBLIOGRAPHY

Jeff Archer, *The NLP Diet*, Teach Yourself (Hodder & Stoughton, 2011)

Richard Bandler and John Grinder, *Frogs into Princes* (Real People Press, 1981)

Steve Bavister and Amanda Vickers, *NLP*, Teach Yourself (Hodder & Stoughton, 2004)

Steve Bavister and Amanda Vickers, *Essential NLP*, Teach Yourself (Hodder & Stoughton, 2010)

Richard Churches and Roger Terry, *NLP for Teachers* (Crown House, 2007)

Judith DeLozier and John Grinder, *Turtles All the Way Down* (Grinder & Assoc., 1995)

Bekki Hill, *NLP for Writers*, Teach Yourself (Hodder & Stoughton, 2013)

Sue Knight, *NLP at Work* (Nicholas Brealey, 2009)

Sue Knight, *NLP Solutions* (Nicholas Brealey, 1999)

James Lawley and Penny Tompkins, *Metaphors in Mind* (The Developing Company Press, 2000)

Jeremy Lazarus, *Ahead of the Game* (Ecademy Press, 2006)

Joseph O'Connor, *Free Yourself from Fears* (Nicholas Brealey, 2005)

Joseph O'Connor, *NLP Workbook* (HarperCollins, 2001)

Joseph O'Connor and John Seymour, *Introducing NLP* Thorsons, 2003

Romilla Ready and Kate Burton, *Neuro-Linguistic Programming for Dummies* (John Wiley, 2010)

Virginia Satir, *The Satir Model* (Science and Behaviour Books, 1991)

Mo Shapiro, *Successful Neuro-linguistic Programming In A Week*, Teach Yourself (Hodder & Stoughton, 2012)

Adrian Tannock, *Beat Insomnia with NLP*, Teach Yourself (Hodder & Stoughton, 2011)

Lisa Wake, *NLP Principles in Practice* Ecademy Press, 2012

John Whitmore, *Coaching for Performance* (Nicholas Brealey, 2009)

Discover the secrets behind greatness

For more information visit:
www.secretsguides.com